FINISH WHAT YOU STARTED

BEAT PROCRASTINATION, END LAZINESS, GET THINGS DONE AND NEVER RELAPSE

MATT ROSEN

COPYRIGHT

Copyright © 2022 Matt Rosen

All rights reserved. No part of this book may be reproduced or used in any manner without the prior written permission of the copyright owner, except for the use of brief quotations in a book review.

To request permissions, contact the publisher at hello@self-improvement.me

ISBN: 979-8-9857158-0-4

First paperback edition: March 2022

TABLE OF CONTENTS

Copyright	2
TABLE OF CONTENTS	3
A Special Gift for You	7
A Quick Note on This Book	9
Introduction	11
Part 1: Know The Enemy	21
Chapter One: Procrastination - A Century-Old Problem	23
What Is Procrastination?	25
Is It Just You?	25
You Are Losing Money (and Your Health)	27
Chapter Two: Separating Facts From Fiction	37
Myths Associated with Procrastination	38
Myth No. 1: It's All About Time-Management	39
Myth No. 2: It's Just Delaying	43

Myth No. 3: Procrastination Means That You're Lazy…	47
Myth No. 4: It's in My DNA	50
A New Approach	51
Part 2: Face The Enemy	55
Chapter Three: Why Are You Stuck?	57
A Tale of Two Fishermen	58
What Causes You to Procrastinate?	59
Prioritizing Our Present Mood	62
Different Causes of Procrastination	63
Type 1: Self-Deception and Planning Failures	63
Type 2: Insecurities	69
Type 3: Motivation and Rewards	75
Chapter Four: Facing Daily Enemies	81
Procrastination: Entering the Maze	83
Anxiety Loops	86
Low Levels of Energy	88
Distractions	89
Not Persevering	92
Procrastination: A Deadly Combination	94
Part 3: Conquer The Enemy	97
Chapter Five: How To Finish What You Started	99
Improving Our Emotional Regulation Skills	100
Becoming Self-Organized	112

Chapter Six: Solutions for Different Types of Procrastinators   119

    Type 1: Self Deception and Planning Failures   120

    Type 2: Fears and Insecurities   125

    Type 3: Lack of Motivation   131

    Bonus Weapons for Beating Procrastination   134

Chapter Seven: You don't hit the gym once and get a six pack   139

    The DIY Option   140

    The Ready-Made Option   144

Conclusion   145

My Little Ask   149

Acknowledgments   150

If you haven't already…   151

Bibliography   152

A SPECIAL GIFT FOR YOU
WANT THESE 2 EBOOKS FOR FREE?

15 Unconventional Habits and Strategies of Successful people
(Oprah Winfrey, Jeff Bezos, Arianna Huffington, Bill Gates...)

No More Distractions: The Easy Trick That Will Stop You From Getting Distracted

To Download the FREE ebooks just scan the QR code:

if the code doesn't work, please email hello@self-improvement.me

Pssst, I'm currently writing my second book (on **why we all struggle to fall asleep…and what to do about it**)! And I'm looking for 50 early readers to get it for FREE before it's published. If you're interested, send me an email at: hello@self-improvement.me

Thanks!

A QUICK NOTE ON THIS BOOK

Hi, this is Matt. Thank you for buying Finish What You Started, it means a lot to me.

I wanted to warn you that the words *procrastination* and *procrastinator* appear a lot in the book. At first, I thought of using synonyms all throughout, but then I decided to employ the actual words as often as they fit, since they are more powerful. At times, I utilized *postponing* or *delaying*, to replace procrastination, when the word would have appeared twice in the same sentence. Similarly, the word *task,* repeated often in the book, is sometimes replaced by *activity* or *project*.

Enjoy reading!

INTRODUCTION

"Much of the stress that people feel doesn't come from having too much to do. It comes from not finishing what they started."

— David Allen

It was mid-February, a few years ago. As a young college student, I had to write a 3000-word essay on *the effectiveness of enhanced cognitive behavioral therapy for eating disorders* for my psychology degree. A week before the deadline, I locked myself in my room, set aside all my other tasks, and opened the word document on my computer. Brimming with confidence, I typed away on the keyboard—*I was off to a good start.*

Six days later, all that I had to show for the time that I'd spent cooped up in my room were a mere 600 words. Yet, my guitar playing skills improved during this time. And I binge-watched some excellent TV shows, even though that wasn't what I'd planned to do. It was only a day before the deadline, when the fear and stress of failing to turn in my essay reached a breaking point, that I raced through the assignment. Fueled by my anxiety, I completed the paper that I'd been putting off for days within a few hours. Was it the best that I could do? Probably not. I'm sure I could have done a better job had I started earlier. Still, despite this realization, I continued to spend most of my college years delaying important assignments and rushing to complete them at the last minute.

The truth is, we've all succumbed to procrastination at one time or another. Studies suggest that 15-20% of adults suffer from chronic procrastination and 25% consider procrastination their defining trait (Steel, 2007). A 2001 study surveyed 308 men and women and found that 50.7% of the participants used the internet to procrastinate. Internet procrastination was linked to the respondent's perception of the web as a source of stress relief, entertainment, and, ironically, an essential tool for self-improvement and learning (Lavoie & Pychyl, 2001).

  The internet boom of the 21st century may have caused a sizable chunk of the population to reach for their mobile phones to scroll away on social media instead of concentrating on getting things done, but procrastination is not a modern-day epidemic. Humans have long suffered from the habit of unnecessarily delaying essential tasks. A cursory look at the past reveals that some of the biggest names in history struggled with procrastination.

The polymath *par excellence*, Leonardo da Vinci, embodied all the attributes of a perfect Renaissance man. He had an impressive knowledge of mathematics, engineering, astronomy and architecture, and an unparalleled contribution to the arts. He was a brilliant sculptor and an extraordinary painter. The murals and paintings he created are a source of awe and wonder, even centuries after his demise.

With countless inventions and incredible pieces of art to his credit, it's hard to imagine the world-renowned genius as a chronic procrastinator. Yet, only few know that most of the projects he worked on were left unfinished as he got sidetracked by new ideas. It took him 16 years to finish the infamous painting *Mona Lisa,* now displayed in the Louvre museum in France, and 13 years to complete *The Virgin of the Rocks* on display at London's National Gallery. *The Adoration of the Magi* and *Jerome in the Wilderness* were both left unfinished, along with the creation of several inventions that he'd sketched out in his notebook.

Nevertheless, Leonardo's accomplishments overshadowed his tendency to leave most tasks unfinished, and he is remembered today for his ingenious inventions and enigmatic paintings. So, should *we* feel guilty about putting off important tasks and scrolling aimlessly on our phones if he could achieve so much, despite chronic procrastination? Leonardo himself was quick to defend his blatant disregard for deadlines. He is quoted as saying: "Men of lofty genius sometimes accomplish the most when they work the least, for their minds are occupied with ideas and the perfection of their conceptions, to which they afterward give form."

Leonardo's story may have you convinced that procrastination is nothing to worry about. But before you close this book, decide to forget all about the project that's due tomorrow and spend the rest of the day lounging on the couch watching Netflix (hoping that you'll uncover your latent genius like da Vinci), have a look at the results of a 1997 study published on *Psychological Science*. Researchers Diane Tice and William Baumeister noted how frequently college students delayed tasks by rating them on an established scale of procrastination. They also observed their stress levels, academic performance, and overall health throughout the semester. Students who indulged in procrastination, initially seemed to benefit from putting off their work and opting to engage in leisure activities instead, and experienced lower stress levels than other students. However, as the semester progressed, the temporary benefits of procrastination paled compared to the cost of constantly delaying work. The students who procrastinated more, scored lower grades and reported feeling higher stress levels as deadlines loomed near. They also experienced worse health, illnesses and consistently turned in work of subpar quality.
Subsequent research, published in the *Journal of Research in Personality* in 2000, explored the ill effects of procrastination by inviting college students into a lab and asking them to perform a math puzzle. Some participants were told that the task was a meaningful test that would assess their cognitive abilities. Others that

the task was of no real consequence and was designed simply for fun. All the participants were given an interim period before beginning the task, during which they could either prepare for it or kill time by playing games like Tetris. Surprisingly, chronic procrastinators only avoided practicing for the puzzle when they were told that it would be used for their cognitive evaluation. When the task was described as fun and meaningless, the procrastinators acted no differently than the other participants. This led researchers to liken procrastination to self-sabotage, describing it as self-defeating behavior (Jaffe, 2013).

Joseph Ferrari, professor of Psychology at DePaul University and a pioneer of modern research on procrastination, believes that the habit of avoiding important tasks results from a "maladaptive lifestyle". "The chronic procrastinator, the person who does this as a lifestyle, would rather have other people think that they lack effort than lacking ability", he says.

So, if you had high hopes of painting the next Mona Lisa while avoiding an important task, considering the above research it's best to put your paint brush down and finish reading this book first. Anomalies, like Leonardo da Vinci, of individuals who achieved spectacular feats despite engaging in self-defeating behavior like procrastination certainly exist in history. It's important, though, to keep in mind that they make up a tiny fraction of historical figures who achieved something worthwhile.

The chances of you achieving a similar success while procrastinating are extremely slim. You can either go on delaying the tasks on your day's agenda in the vague hope that somewhere between Netflix and doodling on the corners of your notebooks you'd stumble upon a genius idea that changes the course of the rest of your life. Or you can make an active effort to understand exactly *what* causes you to procrastinate and get rid of the habit altogether, so you can reduce stress and perform your best.

It wasn't until I graduated and started my first job that I realized I was suffering from chronic procrastination. It was affecting my life in more ways than I'd imagined. During a stay in Portland, Oregon, determined to change my ways and aiming to become more productive, I made a stop at Powell's. Going through the aisles of the popular bookstore, I bought almost every self-help book I could find. A month later, the books remained untouched on my bookshelf, collecting dust while I continued to procrastinate. I forced myself to read through the first half of a few of the books I'd bought and even felt a brief spark of enthusiasm as I learned different tips to kick procrastination to the curb. Yet, I only found them to be effective for a few days before returning to my old ways.

Fed up with the stress that comes part and parcel with procrastination, I finally decided to carry out my own research and uncover exactly why I continued to behave the way I did. And why I kept setting myself up for failure by putting off things for the eleventh hour.

My perception of procrastination and its causes changed drastically as I delved deep into the topic. Until this point, I had erroneously believed that it was simply an inability to manage priorities and organize oneself in a manner that allows us to make the most of our time. "Procrastination really has nothing to do with time-management," claims Professor Ferrari. He says that telling a chronic procrastinator to *simply* get up and get things done is the same as asking an individual diagnosed with clinical depression to *simply* cheer up.

It turns out, the real reason for procrastination is not an inability to divide our day into neat little portions, dedicating a particular amount of time to a particular task or lacking the motivation to get things done. A growing body of research suggests a strong link between procrastination and a failure to regulate our emotions. Let me state it again: we don't procrastinate because we are bad at time management; we procrastinate because we can't regulate our emotions. All these years, I kept running into dead ends, trying to defeat my chronic procrastination. I would experience short bursts of energy after reading online or in books tips and tricks to kill it, but find myself standing back at square one a few days later, caught up in ennui and sluggishness. Hence why over the years I've learned not to rely on "quick fixes" to solve my problems. Finish What You Started (FWYS) is, in fact, a comprehensive guide for people looking to get rid of procrastination once and for all.

Through this book, you will become familiar with the science behind procrastination while learning the essential life skill of regulating your emotions. Backed with extensive research on the subject, FWYS will teach you effective methods to eliminate procrastination from your life and make the most of your time and skills. Have you ever postponed working on a task thinking that you have a week to get it finished only to realize it was due the next day? Or ever delayed cleaning your apartment because you didn't "feel like it"? An overconfidence in our future selves to get a task done in unrealistic timings and a false sense of security convince us we have more than enough time on our hands to keep us from getting started.

Another reason for postponing what we ought to do is the misconception that we need to *feel* inspired or motivated to get things done. The purpose of this book is also to debunk the myths associated with procrastination that keep us stuck in a cycle of putting things off to avoid perceived discomfort associated with tasks, which invariably makes them more stressful as we run out of time to get them done.

Finish What You Started is your guide to living life to the fullest by eliminating unnecessary stress and finding joy in getting things done. As you read through it, you will find that getting rid of procrastination is not only a way to become more efficient, it also involves learning to be kind to your future self and forgiving your past self. You will discover how you can maximize joy and fulfillment in your life by changing your perspective.

To begin our journey, we'll take a closer look at what procrastination is *not* in Chapter 1. We're also going to discuss some myths tied to procrastination and how these beliefs have been holding you back from getting rid of it once and for all. So, sit back, relax and keep on reading to discover what life would look like when you no longer have the guilt and shame of missing deadlines weighing you down ever again.

PART 1: KNOW THE ENEMY

CHAPTER ONE: PROCRASTINATION - A CENTURY-OLD PROBLEM

"What may be done at any time will be done at no time."
— Scottish Proverb

Once upon a time, there was a famous Zen master named Ryutan. People traveled from distant lands to seek his counsel and learn from his wisdom. One day a scholar named Tokusan, who wanted to learn the secrets of Zen, visited him.

The master watched the keen scholar with great interest as he expressed his desire to learn more about Zen. Over the next few minutes, the master listened quietly to the young scholar as he talked about his ideas, opinions and beliefs about Zen.

As Tokusan rambled on, the Zen master placed an empty teacup before him and started pouring tea from a teapot. The amber liquid filled the cup, but the master continued to pour more until the tea spilled over the cup, flowed down the table and dripped on Tokusan's crisp white robes.

"Stop! The cup is full!" Tokusan yelled as he hurried to clean his robes.

The master put away the teapot, locked eyes with the blabbering scholar and pointed at the cup filled to the brim with tea. "This is you—so full of your own ideas and opinions that there's no room for you to learn anything new. Come back to me with an empty cup."

As we go through life, we fill our cups with our thoughts and perceptions, our experiences and the knowledge we acquire along the way. We unwittingly close ourselves off from learning new ideas and exploring new possibilities.

Before we set off on our journey of understanding why we procrastinate, let's take a few moments to empty our cups and open ourselves to new thoughts and ideas. Martial arts legend Bruce Lee summed it up best when he said: "Empty your cup so that it may be filled; become devoid to gain totality."

What Is Procrastination?

The word "procrastination" comes from the Latin verb *procrastinare,* which means "to put off work until the next day". It also has roots in the Greek term *Akrasia,* which was used to describe the state of acting against one's own better judgment.

In modern times, we can define procrastination as voluntarily delaying action on a given task despite the knowledge that we'd be worse off because of the delay. Dr. Piers Steel, professor of motivational psychology at the University of Calgary, puts it rather bluntly by defining procrastination as "self-harm".

Is It Just You?

Present-day generations enjoy incredible ease of access to information and entertainment. It's tempting to credit our short attention spans and lack of persistence to the advent of the internet. However, it becomes evident when we look back on past civilizations that humankind has struggled with a habitual hesitation to get things done since ancient times. In 700 BC, the Greek poet Hesiod painstakingly worked away on his stone tablet instructing future generations not to "put your work off till tomorrow or the day after". The high-ranking Roman consul Cicero termed procrastination as "hateful" when it came to running government affairs.

Today, nearly 20% of men and women in America reportedly suffer from chronic procrastination. This is higher than the percentage of people diagnosed with clinical depression or various phobias. It gives us an idea of exactly how common it is to keep putting things off. So it seems the warnings of ancient sages against the evils of procrastination went unheeded.

What makes our tendency to delay important tasks even more interesting is the aspect of "self-awareness" tied to it. The delay is not something that just happens: we not only *know* that we are avoiding a task, we are also aware that we would most likely suffer as a result. Yet, we continue to do it anyway. Researchers believe, in fact, that procrastination is an "essentially irrational" habit. Since the human brain is programmed for survival, it makes little sense to do something that we know would harm us in the long run. Which leads us to the question: *why* do we continue to procrastinate? Procrastination is often viewed as a time-management problem, and individuals who procrastinate are often regarded as lazy or unmotivated. However, researchers believe that postponing is not a distinct character flaw or a result of poor time-management skills, but a coping mechanism we employ to deal with negative emotions associated with tasks such as fear, self-doubt, boredom, frustration and insecurity. We're going to discuss the causes of procrastination and understand exactly what's going on in our brain that makes us put things off for later in Chapter 2. For now, let's have a look at exactly what procrastination costs us.

You Are Losing Money (and Your Health)

Author of *Massive Life Success* and founder of *Procrastinate Zero*, Darius Foroux, surveyed 2,219 individuals and found that nearly 88% of people in the workforce procrastinate one to four hours daily on average. Looking at these figures, you are bound to think to yourself that if almost everyone procrastinates, then why does it matter? Let's have a look on what this means.

By wasting 3 hours each day, a person with an annual income of $40,000 loses nearly $15,000. Thus, constantly delaying tasks to pursue more pleasurable activities not only affects your performance, it impacts how much money you make. A study performed by Brenda Nguyen at the University of Calgary corroborates these findings and suggests that high levels of procrastination are linked to low salaries, shorter employment periods and a high probability of staying unemployed. The study also found that women overall procrastinated less often than men and explored the effect of the work environment on an employee's ability to retain attention. The research shed light on the fact that procrastinators were less likely to hold on to jobs that required a high level of motivation, but also emphasized the fact that certain jobs could foster procrastination.

Whether low rewarding jobs or demotivating workplaces are the problem, procrastinators suffer the most by missing out on large sums of potential income.

In addition to creating a gaping hole in your income, procrastination affects your future career prospects as your performance at the workplace declines. A 2018 survey found that procrastination at the workplace negatively affected performance. The study discovered that individuals who had high levels of energy, mental strength and resilience didn't engage in non-work related activities at the workspace as much as the other employees. The researchers noted that people who spent time on personal activities such as reading blogs, browsing through social media and gossiping with other colleagues performed poorly at work compared to the employees who concentrated mostly on their work. The procrastinators consistently turned in low- quality work or failed to get the required amount of work done, leaving most tasks unfinished (Metin et al., 2018). Regularly spending work hours procrastinating means that employees make slow progress at completing a task. As a result, they have to rush to get things done, compromising the quality of the end result.

Avoiding a laborious task gives rise to momentary feelings of relief at first. But all those good feelings go downhill once the deadline for completing the task approaches closer. Dr. Tim Pychyl, Professor of Psychology and a member of the Procrastination Research Group at Carleton University in Ottawa, led a 2013 study which found that procrastinators opted for short-term mood repair over long-term satisfaction that arises through the achievement of one's goals. If all that wasn't enough to convince you to get off the couch and get started on that assignment you've been putting off for weeks, then let's have a closer look at some of the negative impacts that habitual procrastination can have on your health.

How Procrastination Is Affecting Your Health

Delaying an important work assignment while you engage in water cooler conversation with your colleagues or play solitaire on your computer may seem harmless, but it's causing you to fall behind and lose out on making money. The habit of putting things off for later not only makes you earn less, it also affects your mental and physical health by inviting stress, guilt, shame and fear into your life.

Sleep Deprivation

Ever laid down on bed at night hoping to catch up on some much needed sleep... only to find yourself lying awake with your eyes wide open as you scroll aimlessly through Instagram and Facebook? Somewhere in the back of your mind, you know that you're going to regret this moment when the alarm goes off at 6 in the morning and you have to drag your tired and weary self out of bed.

Sleep procrastination is so common in the US that the Center of Disease Control has gone so far to call it a "public health epidemic". More than a third of the people in the US get less than seven hours of sleep on average and 38% of these sleep deprived individuals are likely to take an unplanned snooze the next day. For many people, avoiding sleep is a way to put distance between them and an undesirable event that may take place the following day, like getting up for work or a presentation that they're not looking forward to. Coincidentally, the electronic devices we reach out for when we want to avoid sleep (mobile phones, laptops and TV) contribute to keeping us awake because of the emission of blue light.

The blue artificial light that these screens emit tricks the brain into thinking it's daytime, which makes us feel more alert and makes sleep a distant possibility. The blue light hitting your eyes sets off a chain of neural activity which disrupts the release of melatonin, the hormone that causes drowsiness and keeps you asleep.

As you scroll away on your phone or watch season after season on your laptop while bundled up in your blanket, with the lights turned off, your body grows tired, but your mind stays wide awake (Weller, 2014). Sleep disorder expert, Dr. Harneet Walia, believes that people should make sleep a priority given the potential health risks associated with lack of adequate rest. "We always recommend a good diet and exercise to everyone, but along the same lines we recommend proper sleep as well," she says in *Here's What Happens When You Don't Get Enough Sleep (And How Much You Really Need a Night)*. Here are some problems associated with poor sleep patterns:

- Excessive drowsiness throughout the day.
- Reduced ability to recall memories, remember and process information.
- Mood swings and lack of alertness.
- Increased risk of running into car accidents (the National Highway Traffic Safety Administration reports that drowsy drivers account for thousands of car injuries and crashes each year).
- Potential health problems associated with chronic sleep disorder include the risk of developing diabetes, high blood

pressure, heart failure or stroke and an increased likelihood of becoming obese, suffering from depression and decreased immunity.

Binge Eating

Your seemingly harmless habit of putting things off for later is not only making you lose money, it's also causing you to put on a few extra pounds.

A group of researchers in China surveyed 1013 college students, and respondents were divided into two groups: binge eaters and non-binge eaters, based on the scores on a binge eating scale (BES). The researchers explored the relationship between binge eating and decision-coping patterns, as well as monetary decision making. The participants were asked to take multiple tests and questionnaires to assess their decision-making skills. Compared to the non-binge eating group, binge eating individuals showed poor decision-making skills and high levels of procrastination.

The research concluded that there was a strong link between binge eating and procrastination, and procrastinators are at a higher risk of developing overeating behavior (Yan et al., 2018). The reason procrastinators can't stop munching on chips and chugging down big bottles of soda is that procrastination results from defective decision-making, which also triggers other addictive behaviors such as gambling or alcoholism.

Procrastination Linked to Poor Health

If you have developed a habit of delaying every task that comes your way, then chances are you're delaying your all-important visits to the doctor. A 2003 study led by Professor Tim Pychyl and Fuschia Sirios explored the negative health consequences of procrastination. The researchers found that procrastination was not only linked to stress but also stimulated a behavioral pathway that caused poor overall health and delay in seeking treatment for illnesses. The study concluded that habitual delay led to an increased vulnerability for negative health outcomes.

Postponing important activities also causes poor mental health since procrastinators experience elevated stress levels, show a deep concern to feel socially desirable and delay seeking therapy for their deteriorating mental health.

Who Is This Book for?

After graduating from college, I immediately enrolled myself in a one-year graphic design course, although I didn't have such a strong passion for it. I was unconsciously terrified of starting out in my career. I felt like I'd been thrust into the real world too soon and because I feared I didn't have what it takes to make it, I avoided applying for full-time positions by studying something else while working afternoons in a coffee shop.

Like I mentioned before, procrastination is a way for us to deal with discomfort associated with certain tasks and avoid feeling negative emotions. In my case, it was the belief that I wasn't good enough. I was so terrified of the real world confirming my belief that I avoided applying for jobs in my field and wasted twelve months pursuing a diploma course I had little interest in.

Procrastination makes us do some incredibly strange things we might look back on years later and wonder exactly why we did that. But, just like most of how we choose to procrastinate make little sense (like feeling a sudden urge to learn to juggle or memorize the lyrics to a rap song when your time would be better spent preparing for an exam), sometimes we engage in rather productive tasks when we're procrastinating.

In the book *The Art of Procrastination,* philosopher John Perry talks about "structured procrastinators". He defines them as individuals who avoid a particular task by being productive on something else. For instance, if these people have 10 items on their to-do list and *number 1*, the most important, is a complicated task, they concentrate and accomplish the remaining 9 items, in an effort to avoid the difficulties hidden behind the first one. The upside of structured procrastination is that these individuals use their time productively and still achieve *something*. However, the downside of this form of procrastination is that we can almost always find something else that we would convince ourselves of as more important just so that we could avoid the biggest task on the list.

Renaissance artist Leonardo da Vinci was a prime example of a structured procrastinator. British art historian Kenneth Clark called him "the most relentlessly curious man in history". For example, when he was commissioned by the Duke of Milan to create the world's largest equestrian statue, he decided he needed to learn the correct anatomy of horses to craft a lifelike statue. So he set off to dissect several horses and made a series of detailed diagrams, sketches, drawings and charts. The biographer, Walter Isaacson, described the sketches as art interwoven with science. Regardless of how spectacular the diagrams were in the end, he never got around to creating the statue he had originally set out to create. He became so engrossed in his research that he began writing a treatise on the anatomy of horses and started planning to make the stables cleaner. He also designed several systems for mangers by devising mechanisms to refill feed bins through conduits from an attic and clean manure, with the help of water showers and an inclined floor. As for the statue he was commissioned to create, Leonardo only got around to making a clay model, which was later destroyed.

Structured procrastinators generate positive feelings as they feel a sense of achievement by crossing off other items on their to-do list, but these feelings are usually short-lived and they experience mounting stress as the task that they'd been avoiding finally looms closer. The longer they avoid working on a particular task, the more it piles up while they run out of time to complete it.

If you're someone who struggles consistently with delaying tasks, then the stress brought on by finishing your work at the last minute probably made you promise yourself to get rid of the habit a couple of times. It may have caused you to deactivate your social media accounts, get rid of your PlayStation and lock yourself in your room determined to finish what you started... only to find that even after spending many hours on a project, you have achieved nothing worthwhile. You may scratch your head at the end of the day and wonder why you weren't able to get yourself to finish a task, even after getting rid of all possible distractions.

The answer is that even though distractions play a huge role in making you put things off for later, they aren't the sole cause of procrastination. Your determination to kick this bad habit may have caused you to look it up on the internet and read a number of articles to help you get rid of it. But no matter what you do, you always find yourself back at square one: unable to finish what you started. This is because many of the things you read online are just myths. In Chapter 2, we're going to look at some of these myths and separate fact from fiction.

Key Takeaways

1. Empty your cup and open yourself to new ideas.
2. Humans have been procrastinating for centuries to avoid negative emotions.
3. Procrastination is a "mood regulating" mechanism.
4. Delaying tasks for later makes you lose money, gain weight, miss out on sleep and delay seeking treatment for your health.
5. What you *think* procrastination is could just be a myth.

CHAPTER TWO: SEPARATING FACTS FROM FICTION

"The great escape of our times is escape from personal responsibility for the consequences of one's own behavior."
— Thomas Sowell

A university professor walked into his class one day holding a big glass jar in his hand. On his desk was an assortment of different items: pebbles, sand, and rocks. The curious students watched on as he proceeded to fill the jar with the rocks. Once the jar was full of rocks, he looked at the students and asked whether they thought the jar was full. The group of students eagerly nodded.

He then picked the bowl of pebbles and poured them over the rocks. The pebbles tumbled between the rocks, sliding between the rocks.

When all the pebbles had filled the jar, he asked the same question again: was the jar full? The students exchanged confused looks with each other and nodded their heads once more.

The professor smiled and then picked up the bowl of sand, pouring it over the rocks and pebbles. The fine grains of sand filled the small spaces between the empty spaces and the bowl was soon empty. With the jar filled to its maximum capacity, the professor turned to the class and explained that if he had started by filling the jar with sand, there would have been no room left for the pebbles or the rocks.

In the same way, if we spend all our time and resources on inconsequential activities, we'll have no time or energy left for the crucial tasks that could have an enormous impact on our life. In the end, we will simply be left with regret as we look back on life and imagine what it would've been like if we hadn't missed those opportunities.

In the last chapter, we learned exactly what procrastination is. Now let's look at what it is not.

Myths Associated with Procrastination

There are a lot of misconceptions tied to procrastination in our society. Almost all of these are based on the concept of viewing *procrastination* as a fundamental flaw in one's personality. While procrastination is a result of defective decision-making, and people with certain personalities are prone to it more than others (for example perfectionists, people pleasers and people with low self-esteem), it is not just limited to one's personality. There are several factors that contribute to making people procrastinate.

We will discuss the reasons behind procrastination in later chapters, for now let's focus on eliminating some myths associated with the perpetual habit of indulging in delays, since some of these beliefs aim at shaming the procrastinator and give rise to even more negative emotions which only makes it more difficult to get rid of the habit altogether.

Myth No. 1: It's All About Time-Management

Does it ever feel like that no matter what you do, you just don't have enough time? Living in the age of technology, we enjoy the luxury of working from the comforts of our homes. On average, more people work today over the weekend and late at night than ever before. The number is particularly high in America as compared to other countries.

A 2017 survey performed by Gallup of 15000 Americans found that 43% of the respondents spent at least some of their time working remotely, marking a 4% increase from 2012. Americans are also working more frequently from home; almost 4 to 5 times a week, a sharp increase since 2012, when people reported working remotely for only a day or just a few hours in a week. And since the Covid-19 pandemic, numbers have only gone up. With all the time we save from working remotely, by reducing the number of hours spent commuting and the flexibility that home working allows us, you would think that present-day generations would enjoy more free time. Yet, that is definitely not the case.

People today find themselves hard pressed to find free-time, even though we are now working far less than we ever did before. The average number of hours that Americans work today in a week is 34 hours compared to the 38-hour long work week in 1964. If we go a little further back in time, then the average work week for manufacturing employees in the 1860s was 62 hours, while in the 1600s, the Puritanical belief that "idle hands are the devil's worship" caused people to work from sunrise to sunset (Hargreaves, 2013).

While people continue to report feeling like they don't have access to enough free time, the reality is quite the opposite. In 1965, Americans spent almost 35 hours a week out of their offices and doing non-work related activities at home such as housework, cooking and sleeping. According to the Bureau of Labor Statistics, this number has shot up in recent times and Americans now get at least 42 hours each week.

Remote working and a boom in part-time jobs may have contributed to lowering these figures. Also, it is important to remember that today's generations have a leg up due to access to electronic gadgets and devices, which save a significant amount of time that would otherwise be spent on cooking, cleaning and doing other household chores. "I just can't find the time" is a common excuse that we use when we can't seem to get ourselves to do something, but keeping the above statistics in mind, it seems that *time,* or not having enough of it, is not the problem.

Professor Ferrari insists that a lack of time management is not what causes procrastination. "We cannot manage time; time is and cannot be controlled," he says. "We can only manage ourselves and how well we fit into time." We often end up believing that procrastination entails that we are not organized enough or that we are bad at planning and managing our time properly.

Let's revisit the example of Leonardo da Vinci, one the most famous procrastinators ever. Matteo Bandello, an Italian writer and monk of the 16th century, observed the great painter while he worked on *The Last Supper*, which took him three years to finish. Bandello noted that at times he would arrive at sunrise and spend the entire day working on the painting, often forgetting to drink or eat in the process. Other times, he would spend several hours standing before his unfinished work, examining and grousing over small details. In those days, he would not bother picking up a brush and would make no progress. Then there were times when the Italian polymath would be busy working on another project, and all of a sudden feel the urge to abandon it and rush to the painting of *The Last Supper*. He would hurriedly climb up the scaffolding, add one or two brushstrokes, then leave.

The moments that Leonardo spent standing before the painting, gazing up at the mural, criticizing the work that he'd done so far, and planning what needed to be done, may have helped him create a masterpiece that withstood the test of time. But my guess is that you're not working on a mural commissioned by the Duke of Milan.

You're just trying to convince yourself to get off the couch and get started on that assignment you've been putting off for weeks or finally write down a business model for your startup.

While being organized certainly helps to get things done, obsessing over planning, organization and analyzing every minute detail of a project before you begin working on it is another way of procrastinating.

When I was a college student, I found some courses extremely complicated. The fear that I wouldn't be able to pass them lingered in the back of my mind all semester. One day, as I walked into a bookstore, I found a manual aimed at college students to help them prepare for their exams. I convinced myself that I'd found the solution to all my problems and bought it. Over the next few weeks, I read the book and learned about how I could organize each subject into different topics and then subtopics, and create a detailed schedule to achieve my desired target within a certain timeframe.

You can probably imagine my frustration when, after weeks of drawing up charts to track my progress and meticulously designing time tables for studying, I barely managed to pass my exam. Spending all that time organizing and preparing for studying was somewhat fun, and it gave me a false sense of confidence that I was doing well in my studies. But I was simply procrastinating.

Most of us end up believing that our habit of procrastination would magically disappear if we could just get better at planning and organizing our calendars. Sadly, the reason we don't finish what we started is embedded deep within our minds.

Myth No. 2: It's Just Delaying
"I'll get around to it."

That's one phrase that every procrastinator is bound to have used one time or another. So what if the Christmas tree is still up even though it's almost July? Why does it matter that you still haven't mowed the lawn and it's almost 8-inches tall? You'll get around to it, eventually. You'll get the job done even if it takes you twice the amount of time it would take any other person, but what matters is that *you'd get it done*. Those are some of the excuses we tell ourselves to make us feel a little better about our procrastination.

Other times, we'll convince ourselves that the delay is absolutely necessary. You just *have* to spend weeks researching the topic thoroughly before you start writing the assignment. You must gather as much information as you can about your new business idea to ensure it's a success. You can't possibly get started on that DIY project before watching at least a dozen tutorials on YouTube. You may even convince yourself that the stress that comes from doing things at the last moment is good for you and makes you perform better.

It took me years to get rid of these self-defeating beliefs and practices that made me cling on to my delaying tactics. Remember that in order to fix a problem, you must first know that a problem exists. I mentioned earlier that the most interesting aspect of procrastination is "self-awareness". While we are aware of the harm we're inflicting upon ourselves by procrastinating, we justify our behavior to lessen our feelings of guilt and shame. Minimizing the consequences of our actions and deluding ourselves into thinking that we're, in fact, better off procrastinating is simply living in denial.

Excessively Researching a Task Before Attempting It
Gathering all the information available before embarking on a course of action is the hallmark of good leadership. However, procrastinators use it to stall making decisions and free themselves of responsibility for how things turn out. Professor Ferrari calls procrastination a *social esteem* issue. "Procrastinators say, 'If I never finish a task, you can't judge me as being incompetent,'" he states. "They would rather have the negative public image that they lack *effort* than *ability*. Lacking effort implies that they might have the ability, and that's not as damaging as lacking skills." What sets procrastination apart from good leadership is that the former is centered around our ego and our need to protect ourselves, while the latter is an act of selflessness. Good leadership is about making sure that we use all the resources available to make the best decision for others. Procrastination is a way for us to gain temporary relief and try to free ourselves from taking responsibility for not performing our best (Vozza, 2015).

The Effect of Stress on Performance

"I do things at the last minute because I perform well under stress."

There was a time when I could've sworn that the unnecessary delay helped me perform better. Over the years, I've met a number of people who believe the same. Having held the same belief for a good part of my life, I can understand where it comes from.

Think back to the last time that you didn't get around to doing a school assignment or a project till the night before the deadline or a few hours before your teacher walked into class to collect your work. The adrenaline pumping inside your blood vessels made you pick up the pen, and you watched it race across the paper as you jotted down a hundred words per minute. Just a few days earlier, you had sat on your chair and stared at the blank sheet of paper before you for hours. Seeing yourself now, as you write at lightning speed - you're blown away. You manage to scribble in the last few words as the door opens and your teacher walks in.

Finally, as you hand in your paper, you feel a sense of satisfaction and relief wash over you. Looking around you see other students turning in the assignments they'd taken a week to write, but you just did it in a mere few hours and a smug smile creeps up over your lips. You feel a bit like a superhero.

Now, whether the paper gets you a low grade or you barely manage to pass - it doesn't matter. Whatever the outcome, it will always exceed your expectations because you completed a task designed for a week in only an hour.

A 2001 experiment published in The European Journal of Personality aimed at bursting the bubble that procrastinators live in that stress aids their performance. A group of procrastinators and non-procrastinators were asked to perform a series of tasks under cognitive stress while their speed and the number of errors they made was recorded. The researchers noted that procrastinators did not only perform the tasks slower than the non-procrastinators, they also made more errors. This led the researchers to conclude that chronic procrastinators were ineffective in regulating their speed and accuracy when they performed under pressure (Ferrari, 2001).

Furthermore, a research published in the Psyhconomic Bulletin and Review in 2006 showed that even individuals with high working memory capacity, if under stressful conditions, performed worse at math problems that they otherwise could have solved with ease (Gimming et al., 2006).
Now that we've established that no one works better under stress, let's rephrase the above quote so that it reflects the truth about procrastination. "I do things at the last minute because if I don't perform well, then I have the excuse of not having enough time to do my best."

Earle Hagen, the acclaimed Hollywood music composer, believed that we can cultivate the mental discipline required to meet deadlines and turn it into a habit through regular practice. He wrote the following statement in his 1990 book titled Advanced Techniques for Film Scoring: "The mental discipline necessary to work toward a deadline is something that you must develop. It can become a habit just as letting things slide until the last minute can become a habit. That pattern leads to staying up all night and writing in a blind panic. Besides ruining your health, you never can write your best. If anyone tells you, 'I have to wait until the pressure is on before I can start to cook', don't believe it. Occasionally, you may be able to work under pressure of a deadline, but stop kidding yourself, it won't be your best."

Myth No. 3: Procrastination Means That You're Lazy and Undisciplined

For a long time, procrastination was confused with laziness or being undisciplined. Even today, these attributes are used to identify procrastinators. While laziness bolsters some people to put off doing things for later, it makes little sense to bunch all procrastinators and place them under the lazy label.

Most individuals do not finish what they started only in some areas of their lives, while they continue to perform well in others. One person may avoid unpleasant work assignments by organizing the clothes in their closet. Someone else may choose to work on an assignment and avoid the jumbled pile of clothes in the closet. Most procrastinators avoid a task they perceive as difficult or complicated by keeping themselves occupied with something else rather than sitting idle. Laziness is not the actual cause behind procrastination, but a symptom for negative emotions such as fear, anxiety, insecurity and stress.

Lack of Discipline

It's a common misconception that procrastinators lack self-discipline. We discussed in the beginning of this book that *finishing what we started* has nothing to do with self-control but everything to do with regulating our emotions. Many people who continue to delay a task will display extraordinary amounts of discipline in other areas of their life. For example, a person procrastinating filing their tax return may spend the evening doing laundry, neatly folding all their clothes and arranging them according to color in the closet. All that requires *discipline*. If such a person invited you to their house, you'd stare in awe at how tidy and organized everything is and compliment them over their remarkable self-discipline.

If you start believing that your procrastination is a result of not having enough discipline, chances are you are going to exacerbate negative feelings about yourself. Thus leading to more procrastination in the future. There is an entire body of research focused on the negative thoughts associated with procrastination called "procrastinatory cognitions inventory (PCI)". These thoughts generate elevated levels of distress and stress, which causes us to postpone an activity. A paper published in 2012 found a strong link between PCI and experiencing negative thoughts, reflecting a low level of self-actualization, apprehensions about a task, perfectionism and imposter syndrome.

The negative feelings that follow procrastination motivate us to seek temporary relief, making us procrastinating even more. This is what makes the cycle so vicious. Putting things off rewards us in the immediate present and once we're rewarded for doing something, we feel a strong urge to repeat the same behavior in the future.

Chronic procrastination costs us our productivity in the present and slowly erodes our mental and physical health over time. It causes us to experience chronic stress, psychological distress, depression, decreased life satisfaction, hypertension, anxiety, poor health behaviors and cardiovascular diseases.

Wait... wasn't procrastination supposed to make you feel better? If procrastination makes you feel worse in the long run, then what's the point of avoiding a task that would cause you moderate amounts of distress and opting for delay that would most likely make you feel more distressed later on?

Turns out we have evolution to thank for our habit of putting our future selves in jeopardy. The human brain is hard-wired to prioritize short-term gains over the fulfillment of long-term goals. A phenomenon known as *present bias*. It is a process that helped our ancestors survive in the wild by prioritizing hunting for food or fighting off predators to take care of their needs in the present.

Psychologist and professor of Marketing at the UCLA Anderson School of Management, Dr. Hal Herschfield extensively researched how we project ourselves in the future. His research led him to the discovery that we tend to see our future selves as "strangers". So when we're putting things off for later, a part of us thinks that the unpleasant tasks that we're delaying, and the negative feelings that are sure to follow as a result of our procrastination, are somebody else's problems (Leiberman, 2019). Moreover, our ability to form thoughtful and future-oriented decisions becomes even more compromised when we are feeling stressed.

So procrastination is not a simple case of simple laziness or lack of self-discipline. There are several neural and behavioral factors at play that lead us towards it.

Myth No. 4: It's in My DNA

We get a pre-packaged set of problems in life from our parents in the form of genes. It's tempting to look at them and hold them responsible for our inability to finish what we started as well. After all, it's been six months since your mom started painting the walls of the guestroom and she's still not finished. While dad still hasn't gotten around to fixing the fence. You inherited your short-sightedness and lactose-intolerance from them, so it only makes sense that your habit of procrastination came from them too.

While your genes are indeed the reason you have to wear glasses or you can't consume dairy, *procrastination* is not. It is a learned behavior and not something that you have to struggle with for the rest of your life because you were born with it. Although a recent study from the University of Edinburgh draws similarities between procrastination and impulsivity, and suggests that it could be hereditary in some individuals, experts in the field like Professor Joseph Ferrari vehemently reject the research calling it "flawed" and "dangerous" (Archontaki et al., 2013). If the problem is genetic, then there is no reason to change it, he says. He believes that procrastination is a byproduct of our upbringing and our environment, crediting nurture instead of nature for indulging in delaying tactics. So the actual struggle is not laziness or lack of discipline, but trying to get rid of the excuses we use to justify our inefficiency to finish what we started.

A New Approach

In today's fast paced-world, we are all looking for a quick solution to our problems. A magic pill, a shortcut, or an easy fix to help us get rid of a problem, any problem, so that we can move on with our lives. Yet, in reality, shortcuts don't work because they only fix the issue on the surface. They might help alleviate the symptoms, but they can't get to the root of the problem and erase it completely.

Change takes time and effort. There are no shortcuts to make it fast to the finish line. If we want a long-term solution for our procrastination, then we have to ditch the ineffective, *lazy* approach and dive deep into our minds to root out the habit once and for all.
    Even though we are inclined to give priority to short-term gains over long-term satisfaction, we can change our mindset and become

more goal-oriented. An excellent example of giving preference to long-term growth over short time benefits is the business tycoon Jeff Bezos. The Wall Street group famously derided Amazon's humble quarterly earnings. However, Bezos ignored the criticism levied against him by financial analysts and focused on the company's long-term plans. At the time of writing, Amazon is the biggest company in the world, making Jeff Bezos the richest person alive.

The company's success was in part due to the fact that Bezos didn't let short-term profits derail his long-term goals. Instead of worrying about the company's quarterly performance, he concentrated on generating profits five, ten, and twenty years down the road.

So the best way to tackle the enemy within and get rid of procrastination is to change our perspective. Start focusing on long-term benefits rather than getting distracted by short-term pleasures. In Part 2, we will learn how to fight *this* enemy. Since the first step of going up against it is to know everything we can about it, let's now look at the actual causes that prevent you from finishing what you started.

Key Takeaways

1. Procrastination is a coping mechanism for emotion regulation. It is not a time-management problem.
2. There is no such thing as performing well under stress. Stress negatively affects performance for everyone.

3. Procrastinators perform worse under stress than non-procrastinators, but they cannot assess their performance accurately, which causes them to believe that they did well.
4. Procrastination is not related to laziness or lack of self-discipline.
5. It is centered around protecting our ego from coming to terms with uncomfortable truths about ourselves.
6. It causes short-term relief, but leads to increased distress later on, which further impairs decision-making in procrastinators and leads to more future delay.
7. It is not a hereditary problem. We learn it from our environment and upbringing.
8. Procrastinators rely on excuses to make themselves feel better.

PART 2: FACE THE ENEMY

CHAPTER THREE: WHY ARE YOU STUCK?

"If you know the enemy and know yourself, you need not fear the result of a hundred battles."

— Sun Tzu

Chinese General and military strategist, Sun Tzu, wrote the advice given above in his famous Art of War in 512 BC. The words still ring true over two thousand years later. He emphasized the importance of familiarizing with what you're up against so that you can build a good strategy targeting your enemy's weaknesses and making the most of your strengths to achieve victory. The same principle applies to our personal lives and the daily challenges we have to face. Because sometimes the enemy lies within us.

The politician, scientist and inventor, Benjamin Franklin, understood this perfectly and often engaged in quiet self-reflection through journaling. Every entry in his journal started with a question: what good do I plan to do today? And ended with a question: what good did I achieve today? He used his journal to hold himself accountable, pinpoint his flaws, correct his behavior and constantly work towards achieving self-improvement.

You can't put up a good fight when you don't even know what you're fighting. You may have determined by now that you struggle to finish what you started, but if you don't know exactly what causes you to procrastinate, you can't win the war. It's impossible to solve a problem without getting to its roots. In this chapter, we are going to look at the different causes that bring people to procrastinate. This will help you identify the reason you keep turning towards procrastination time and again.

A Tale of Two Fishermen

Once, a man headed out to a nearby river to catch fish. He chose a nice spot by the river and set up his fishing equipment and cooking utensils beside him, along with a small makeshift stove for cooking. As he waited for a fish to catch the bait, he noticed another man sitting a few feet away from him holding a fishing rod, with a small stove and a pan.

The first man felt a tug on his fishing rod and quickly reeled in his first catch. He was pleased with the big sized fish he had caught, and stuffed it inside a freezer to cook later. Over the next few hours, the man caught several fish of different sizes and happily stored them in his little freezer. He was ready to start cooking some of the fish when he looked over at the other man and noticed with surprise that he still had caught none.

At that moment, the other man felt a strong tug on his fishing rod and reeled in a huge fish. The first fisherman watched in astonishment as the man looked unimpressed with his catch and tossed it back into the river. The man caught a few more fish over the next few minutes, but each time he released them back into the water. Overcome with curiosity, the first fisherman walked over to the other and asked why he kept putting the fish back into the river. The man pointed to a small cast iron pan that lay by his side and explained that it was because the fish were too big to fit in his pan. Through this entire episode, it did not occur to the second fisherman that he could cut up the fish into small pieces to fit in his pan. Sometimes, we behave like the second fisherman: passing up on opportunities and sabotaging our own progress.

What Causes You to Procrastinate?

Look back on the last time you had to work on an important assignment that you couldn't get yourself to get started on. What exactly stopped you from doing it? It can't be because the latest season of *Money Heist* kept you glued to the screen, even though you may feel tempted to deceive yourself into thinking it was.

Two important traits that are required to keep us focused on completing a task: self-control and motivation. **Negative emotions such as stress, fear and anxiety impede our ability to complete tasks as our bodies seek immediate relief by engaging in activities that deliver instant feelings of gratification. The fault lies in our ability to regulate our emotions and delay gratification.**

Dianne Tice emphasized the role of emotion regulation to achieve self-control in her research paper published in the *Journal of Psychological Inquiry*. She noted that, while emotion regulation was similar to other regulatory tasks, it made up a special case of self-regulation that could hinder self-control. Failure to control our moods and feelings, in particular, led to failure of exercising self-control in other areas of our lives. Usually inhibiting elements such as these manifest because of the following reasons:

Fear of a complex or difficult task and inability to decide where to begin.

Fear of failing at the task.

Losing sight of the reward for completing the task.

The first two cases result from stress and anxiety. The third case happens when our mind fails to consider the reward associated with finishing a task because it seems too far in the future.

When the above factors outweigh our ability to exercise self-control and stay motivated, we turn towards various coping mechanisms to make us feel good and cause temporary relief. To get rid of the stress that our brain associates with a particular task, we start looking for different quick fixes to give ourselves an instant dopamine boost.

If you are someone who struggles to practice emotion regulation, and you are presented with two options to feel good, you will most likely choose the one that delivers a quick reward rather than the one in which the reward lies in the distant future. This is why experts in the field insist that procrastination is not a time-management issue but a failure to regulate our emotions.

In a 2013 research published in the *Journal of Social and Personality Psychology Compass*, researchers Tim Pychyl and Fuschia Sirois concluded that procrastination was a result of self-regulation failure and an inclination towards short-term mood repair. The research focused on the procrastinators' temporal understanding of themselves. It found that a disconnect between the present and future self, made it easier to put things off for later, letting the future self bear the consequences of the delay. This was best illustrated by Homer in an episode of *The Simpsons* in which the lovable character shrugs his responsibilities with the saying: *"That's a problem for future Homer! Man, I don't envy that guy!"*

Prioritizing Our Present Mood

"I'm just going to watch one more episode. It'll put me in a good mood and then I'll be able to finish my assignment in no time."

How many times do we convince ourselves that we need to watch our favorite TV show or use social media before we finish what we started, because it will put us in a better state of mind and energize us?

Most people procrastinate because of a tendency to prioritize their present feelings, even when it comes at the cost of not achieving their long-term goals. A phenomenon termed short-mood repair (Rabin & O'Donoghue, 2000). This form of procrastination is also known as hedonistic delay, in which people succumb to their desires for immediate gratification and engage in behaviors that provide short-term relief. The concept of hedonistic delay is similar to the pleasure principle, which is the tendency to engage in pleasurable activities and ignore unpleasant ones.

The pleasure principle underlines our natural disposition to alleviate our suffering and seek comfort. However, when the instinctive drive to find happiness and soothe pain causes us to pursue short-term satisfaction over the achievement of long-term goals, it becomes a serious problem that affects our ability to succeed in life.

Different Causes of Procrastination

There are different factors that make us less prone to finish what we started. Based on the different reasons behind it, we can classify procrastinators into different types.

Type 1: Self-Deception and Planning Failures

This type includes people who procrastinate because they feel overwhelmed by negative feelings and attitudes they associate with particular tasks. Those tasks cause them to resort to self-deception or rely on a false sense of security to cope with the distress.

Unclear Goals
Compared to clearly defined goals, which create a sense of urgency through deadlines, vague and abstract goals are difficult to achieve. *"I want to lose weight"*, *"I want to get fit"*, *"I want to get better grades"* are all examples of abstract goals that don't specify the exact target. A well-defined goal answers the three big questions: what, when, and how. What do we want to achieve? When do we want to achieve it? And how will we achieve it? If we want to lose weight, a clear and well-defined goal would state exactly the number of pounds that we want to lose by a set time period, and it would outline a plan to achieve our target. For example, *"I want to lose 10 pounds*

by December of this year. I am going to exercise every day for thirty minutes to achieve my goal.

A 2010 article published in the *Psychological Reviews* by social psychologists Yaacov Trope and Nira Liberman presented the concept of *psychological distance*, which can be defined as the extent to which people feel removed from a particular phenomenon. Liberman and Trope believe that psychological distance was primarily egocentric and its reference point is the self in the present moment. The interactions of the self with an object or event that might be removed from the present moment, whether in time, distance or space, determine the level of perceived distance. The two researchers put forth the Construal Level Theory, which states that events that are distant in time are depicted more abstractly in our minds than events that are close in time. For example, if you prepare for a vacation that's in the distant future, you'd feel excitement about your plans as you imagine yourself walking on an exotic beach. But if you had to plan a vacation for next week, then you'd likely spend more time working out the intricate details of your plans like buying tickets, making hotel reservations and planning your itinerary.

The Construal Level Theory implies that goals that seem unrealistic feel abstract, making it unlikely to achieve them. So, if we consider ourselves incapable of achieving a particular outcome, our mind may relegate the task as unimportant and we may feel inclined to ignore it.

Focusing on Future Options

"I'm not procrastinating. I'm just waiting to be older, so I'll be wiser."

Self-deception and procrastination go hand-in-hand. Procrastinators convince themselves that now is not the best time to attempt a particular task. They would be more skilled and better at completing it in the future. They may deceive themselves into thinking they're not in a hurry to do an assignment because it is so easy for them, they could complete it in a short amount of time. They may even tell themselves that an activity would be much simpler and easier to do when they have the right tools available. For example, a procrastinator may avoid committing to the goal of losing weight by telling themselves that they can only lose weight once they have a gym membership. They may waste valuable time waiting to find the right gym and make room in their monthly budget for the membership.

Optimism About the Future

An inflated opinion of one's ability and gross miscalculation of how long it would take them to complete a task can cause people to postpone getting it done when they have the time. In other words, the procrastinator overestimates the abilities of their future self and underestimates the time that it would take for them to finish the task, a phenomenon known as *planning fallacy*.

If a task seems particularly difficult or the person assigned the task struggles to get started, then he or she may delay working and put it off until the next day. Presuming they would be able to get themselves motivated to complete it tomorrow.

A study published in *The European Journal of Personality* in 1989 on Highschool students concluded that procrastinators were more likely to make promises to themselves about things being different in the future. Students responded to a set of questionnaires to measure their anxiety and level of procrastination a week before an exam, on the day of the exam and 5 days later. The results showed that procrastinators felt least challenged 7 days before the exam and resorted to promises and assurances that they would eventually start studying.

Decisions, Decisions, Decisions

Sometimes procrastination boils down to "Indecisiveness". We may face multiple options about how to proceed to finish something we started and find ourselves unable to make a decision. We may vacillate over which course of action we should take or what decision we need to make to actually move on to a general plan of action. Dr. Joseph Ferrari aptly terms this form of procrastination as "the decision not to act." For example, you may find it difficult to get started on your goal of losing weight as you struggle to find the right diet plan. Or you may be unable to decide the topic of your research paper and so delay getting started on the project.

The inability to make a decision when presented with several options is also known as *choice* or *analysis paralysis*. Decision-making may hold you back for several reasons, including the following:

Having more options to choose from makes it difficult for you to make up your mind. Analyzing and evaluating the consequences of each option takes time and can demotivate us from attempting or completing the task.

Options that are similar to each other make it hard for you to decide, especially when no single one stands out in terms of yielding a better outcome.

We may delay deciding when we perceive it as extremely important. The more we consider a decision as having a great impact on our lives, the more we delay making it by overthinking and fixating on making the *right* decision.

Moreover, decision-making chips away at our ability to practice self-control. The more decisions we have to make in a set time period, the more we use up our mental resources, making it difficult to exercise self-control in the future. So, if an activity involves making a lot of decisions, then you may quickly find yourself mentally exhausted, which may lead to more indecisiveness.
 Researcher Timothy Pychyl and Joseph Ferrari performed two studies to analyze the impact of indecision on speed, accuracy and self-control. The results found a negative correlation between

decision making and exercising self-control. This form of procrastination is also known as *decisional procrastination.*

Being Overwhelmed

There are several factors that can lead to overwhelming feelings of anxiety, dread, or fear that cause us to delay working on a project. We might feel overwhelmed when we perceive a particular task as too complicated. A task that involves several smaller activities could also seem daunting and make us more inclined to avoid it altogether. You may perceive the task as too difficult or consider yourself ill-equipped or incapable of getting it completed on time and decide to ignore it to make yourself feel better. The impending task, however, may add to your stress and cause you to become even more anxious than before the longer you delay doing it. This is known as the *feedback loop,* in which anxiety associated with a task causes us to procrastinate, which in turn leads to more anxiety, which manifests in the form of more delays.

For example, if you have to clean the house, you may first start thinking about how long it would take you to finish cleaning everything. Then you may assess how this one mammoth *mission* could be broken into several smaller tasks that you would need to complete. Cleaning your house may entail that you put the clothes in your closet in order as well, scrub the grime in the bathrooms, wash the dishes and finally take down the Christmas decorations that are still up. Thinking about all the numerous sub-tasks you have to achieve in order to complete the big task of cleaning your house may persuade you to give up on the idea altogether. And you may end up settling on the couch and watching *Grey's Anatomy* instead.

Unpleasant Activities

We are more likely to delay doing activities that are unpleasant or unappealing. For example, if you have to make an urgent call to someone you don't like, then you may avoid making that call until the last minute. A 1994 study published in *The Journal of Psychology* on 10th grade students proved the relation between delaying a task and the perception of a task as pleasant or unpleasant. The students were more likely to put off an academic task if they perceived themselves incapable of doing the task and were more likely to change their delaying tactics if they perceived a task as enjoyable (Milgram et al., 1994).

There are several factors that can create aversion towards a particular activity, such as labeling it tedious and frustrating, or because we have doubts about our own competence and perceive it as too difficult for us to handle.

Type 2: Insecurities

Most people want to live with the belief that they are competent and capable of doing something. Hence, they try to avoid having their skills evaluated, as this would shake those beliefs. During my college years, I had developed a habit of starting work on my assignments late and finishing them moments before they were due. The subpar work I turned in often made my professors tell me that I was wasting my potential and, most urgently, that I needed to be more focused. Deep down, I *enjoyed* hearing that and continued to procrastinate. I figured I would rather have people *think* I was capable of so much more than having them conclude once and for all that I wasn't. Procrastination can be a result of our insecurities jumping to the fore, leaving us paralyzed as we struggle with the myriad of negative feelings associated with a particular activity. Some types of insecurities that may render you incapable of getting yourself to finish what you started include:

Fear of Evaluation and Criticism
"We are so scared of being judged that we look for every excuse to procrastinate."
— Erica Jong

I had a friend who kept delaying writing his first book despite bubbling with ideas for the manuscript. Every time I met him, he would tell me about a new story idea that he had and how it was so much better than the last one. His fear of having his work open to criticism and possibly having his pride broken from the negative feedback left him feeling crippled. He never got around to writing that book after all. Usually, the fears that we attach to a particular project are exaggerated and irrational. Most times, the consequences of negative feedback are not as severe as we perceive them to be.

That being said, it is important to note that in some cases the fear of facing negative consequences or punishment acts as motivation to perform our very best and get the job done well before the deadline. Whether fear acts as a motivating or demotivating factor usually depends on people's own ability to deal with anxiety and their level of self-confidence regarding a particular task.

In 2007, a group of researchers analyzed the effect of fear of evaluation on procrastination by examining private university students in Southern California. The research, which was published in *The Journal of Social Psychology*, noted that students with high evaluation threat levels delayed turning in their essays as compared to students with low evaluation threat levels. This led researchers to believe that a significant link existed between feeling threatened by evaluation and performance with the former predicting the latter (Bui, 2007).

Being a Perfectionist
Perfectionism may have helped you score good grades and excel in academia, but it could be the reason you procrastinate. A research from 1999 discovered a strong correlation between perfectionism and anxiety (Onwuegbuzie & Daley, 1999). In fact, an unhealthy obsession with achieving perfection could cause you to wait until you have gathered enough information about a task to get started. It could also cause you to start over and over again in order to perform your best. You may get started on an activity and discard the work you complete because you don't find it good enough and start again.

This may cause you to take much longer than it should, turning you exhausted and mentally frustrated as your performance fails to meet your lofty standards. Your confidence might take a hit and you may give up on thinking that you're no good.

Perfectionism can cause you to become too critical of your work and find faults in everything you do. You may try different methods to get a job done and put in twice the effort to complete a project than what is required. The anxiety associated with being perfect may also cause you to procrastinate and avoid the task. Even if perfectionism may have helped you outshine your peers in some areas, it can prove to be your downfall if your obsession with it makes you lose sight of your target and you keep letting rewards and opportunities slip by.

What If I Won't Succeed?

The all-consuming fear that we might not succeed, that we will be subjected to public embarrassment or shame for not doing a good enough job, can also hold us back from getting started and completing the most important item on our daily agenda. The fear of failing could be so strong that it might stop people from sincerely committing to their dreams and pursuing their goals.

Generally, the more important the task is, the more we are terrified of failing at it. Certain personality traits make some people more prone towards the fear of failure than others. Low self-esteem, low self-confidence and high self-doubts have been found to be associated with fear-based procrastination (Duru & Balkis, 2019).

Interestingly, the fear of failure does not always cause procrastination and might motivate some individuals to launch into action. It leads to procrastination when it decreases people's sense of autonomy or when people deem themselves incapable of dealing with the consequences of the fear. People with a high level of self-efficacy, who have faith in their abilities, are less likely to procrastinate and find that fear motivates them instead.

This type of fear is closely tied with perfectionism and with fear of criticism; however, the presence of one of these traits doesn't mean that the person will be afflicted with the others. Often, procrastinators may suffer from different combinations of these inhibiting factors. For instance, someone with a high level of self-confidence, but with an obsession for achieving perfectionism, may still worry about the criticism that their work would receive.

Self-Sabotaging Ourselves

In some cases, an inclination towards self-defeating behavior causes people to procrastinate. Self-sabotage is usually a result of having low self-esteem. People may fear facing judgments about their capabilities from friends or family members and engage in self-sabotage to protect their ego. Whereas other times it is the need to feel in control that drives people towards self-sabotage. By putting their own chances of success in peril by sabotaging a situation and then rescuing it, people may derive a sense of achievement and temporarily boost their confidence. These quick mood fixes, however, may prove destructive in the long run as they continuously deter people's progress.

People may engage in self-sabotage in different ways. A person may delay applying for a job, forget to prepare for a presentation or repeatedly put off turning in their work assignments. They may block their chances of advancing their careers and pass up on opportunities to get a better job because they believe they deserve to be miserable. Some other ways that people can sabotage their own happiness include getting into toxic relationships and pushing away people who care about them.

Lack of Self-Efficacy

Self-efficacy can be defined as the confidence in our ability to achieve goals. Sometimes the reason people procrastinate is because of a low level of it. If someone believes their chances of completing a project with success are low before they even start doing the first task at hand, then they are more likely to use delaying tactics to avoid it altogether. How capable we view ourselves is different depending on what we are attempting to do. For example, someone who is confident in their academic ability might not possess the same confidence when it comes to sports or vice versa. In some cases, a person who suffers from chronic procrastination may procrastinate even more because they don't believe they can get started on an activity on time. Low self-efficacy in this scenario acts as a self-fulfilling prophecy.

Lack of Self-control

Procrastination can be caused by a feeling of lack of control over our circumstances. If we are convinced that the report we're going to turn in will get criticized by our boss, regardless of how much effort we put into it, we might delay getting started on it. While a perceived lack of control can cause people to procrastinate in specific situations, some people are predisposed to feeling an overall lack of control over their life.

How much control we feel we have over our lives is determined by the locus of control, or the degree to which we believe we can control the events in our life. Our locus of control can either be internal or external. People who are internally oriented tend to focus on things that are directly under their control, such as their moods, feelings, and actions. As a result, they experience having a higher control over their life. People who focus on external factors experience an overall low level of control over their life. They constantly fixate on events that are outside their ability to control, such as other people's opinions, thoughts, their environment or the weather.

Using the earlier example, we will find it easier to get started on a task if we simply focus on giving it our best rather than focusing on how our work would be perceived by our supervisor.

Type 3: Motivation and Rewards

Procrastination can result from low motivation or by losing sight of the reward that awaits us when we finish what we started. Here are the reasons people procrastinate when it comes to motivation and rewards:

Rewards That Seem Too Distant in The Future

Most people discount the value of a particular reward if it lies in the distant future. People usually procrastinate on tasks associated with rewards that they would receive after a long period of time. The *Construal Level Theory* makes these rewards seem abstract and people may feel a sense of disconnect from them because of the perceived psychological distance between themselves and the reward. Attaining a good grade on an exam that is months away may not seem too important to us than getting a good grade on an exam held in a few days. An activity does not register as important enough unless the deadline is looming near and we know exactly what's at stake if we fail.

This is also caused by the *present bias*, which makes us prioritize short-term benefits over the rewards of achieving long-term goals. As humans, we regularly display our present bias by choosing activities that help us feel better in the moment rather than sticking to a plan, such as a work project or a diet, for a long period to reap even greater benefits. An inconsistency is observed between the perceived value of the reward and the time it would take to achieve it. If a reward lies in the distant future, it doesn't matter how long it will take for us to achieve it, we may continue to discount the reward's value. Then a task may finally blip into our radar once we run out of time, and we may no longer ignore the reward attached to its completion.

The same principle applies to punishments. The farther the punishment for failing to complete a task is, the less likely we are to mull over it with seriousness and start working to avoid it.

Feeling Disconnected from Our Future Selves

When I look back on the person I used to be in college, I feel like I barely recognize myself. In the past five years, I reversed my life around and got rid of my habit of procrastination. I often muse meeting my past self and imagine the shock on my younger self's face once they see me. While the likelihood of such a meeting ever taking place is none, it is common knowledge that as we age, we morph into entirely different versions of ourselves. We may seem like a stranger to our past selves.

What's interesting is that while change is inevitable, and most of us are bound to evolve with time, our minds in the present moment feel disconnected from our future selves. A phenomenon known as temporal self-discontinuity or temporal disjunction. In other words, our minds can trick us into thinking that the consequences of our actions or lack of action would be borne by a different person, rather than ourselves, in the future. For example, a person may avoid going on a diet, exercising and eating healthy despite their doctor's warning that their lifestyle choices are affecting their health. They believe it would take a few years for the harmful effects of these choices to manifest. Subconsciously, they may deceive themselves into thinking that the consequences of their sedentary lifestyle and bad food choices would be borne by someone else. That is their future self.

A disconnect between the present and the future selves can cause people to procrastinate in different ways. It can make them think they don't need to worry about the future because someone else will face the consequences of their delay. Also, it can cause people to avoid putting in the effort to get work done because they're not motivated by the reward, believing that someone else would benefit from their hard work.

Low Motivation

Procrastination can also ensue because we don't feel motivated enough to get started on a task. We can define motivation as the force that initiates, guides, and keeps us focused on our goals. It is what spurs us into action, what makes us finish reading a book or complete a work assignment. We can either be intrinsically motivated or extrinsically motivated.

Intrinsic motivation involves feeling driven to complete a task because it feels personally rewarding. It generates a sense of achievement inside us. Extrinsic motivation involves completing a task because of external causes, such as avoiding punishment or gaining rewards. Usually the people who rely on extrinsic motivation to complete a task are more likely to procrastinate than people who feel driven by intrinsic motivation.

In a 2010 article for the Harvard Business Review, Peter Bregman, bestselling author of *18 Minutes*, tells the story of how he helped an elderly man who was struggling to walk in the pouring rain one day. On the other side of the road, he remembers, an Access-A-Ride van for people with disabilities waited for the old man. Its driver, who is actually paid to assist passengers board the vehicle, sitting comfortably inside. The incident left the writer wondering why the driver didn't feel motivated enough to do his job properly even though he was paid for it.

A 2004 research published in the *Journal of Psychological Science* by Dan Ariely and James Heyman sheds some light on this behavior. The researchers asked the participants to use the mouse on the computer screen to drag a circle into a square. A new circle appeared in place of the old one as soon as they finished dragging it into the square. The challenge was to drag as many circles into the box in 5 minutes. The participants were divided into three groups: those who were offered 5 dollars, those who were offered fifty cents, and those who were asked to do the job as a favor. Surprisingly, the group that was asked to complete the task as a favor performed the best, dragging 168 circles. The participants who were offered 5 dollars and 50 cents, dragged 159 and 101 circles, respectively. The results of the experiment showed that individuals perform better when they are intrinsically motivated (altruism being the motivation in this case of the study).

When people are offered rewards for performing a task, they often measure their self-worth against the reward and wonder whether it is worth the effort. This significantly dampens the motivation to succeed and perform to their best abilities (Ariely & Heyman, 2004).

Key Takeaways

1. Procrastination is a result of prioritizing our present moods over long-term achievements.
2. The first step of getting rid of procrastination is to identify the root cause.
3. There are three types of procrastination based on Self-Deception, Insecurities and Motivation & Rewards.
4. Self-deception involves setting abstract goals; becoming overly optimistic about the future, or focusing too much on future options; inability to make a decision; feeling overwhelmed by negative emotions; and task aversion.
5. Procrastination that is driven by insecurities involves engaging in self-sabotage; having low self-efficacy; perceived lack of control over the outcome; fear of failure and fear of evaluation.
6. Procrastination can sometimes be caused by rewards that are too distant in the future or that will be achieved a long time after completing a certain task, as well as by lack of motivation.
7. Motivation can be intrinsic or extrinsic. People who are intrinsically motivated are less likely to engage in delaying tactics than people who rely on extrinsic motivation.

CHAPTER FOUR: FACING DAILY ENEMIES

"I have spent my days stringing and unstringing my instrument, while the song I came to sing remains unsung."
— Rabindranath Tagore

Oda Nobunaga was the greatest Japanese warrior in the 14th century. One day, while he was marching towards the battleground to fight the enemy with his troops, he realized his soldiers were filled with doubt about their victory. They dragged their feet and walked behind him, slumped. Nobunaga stopped on the way to pray at a shrine. His troop waited outside while he went inside the temple to pray. The warrior was certain of his victory, but his soldiers' low morale troubled him. He returned from the shrine and gathered his generals around him. He told them he had an epiphany while he prayed in the shrine: he could find out whether they'd win or lose the battle through a simple coin toss.

The Generals were filled with anticipation as they watched him take a coin out of his pocket and toss it in the air. Nobunaga had told them that if they got heads, they would win. The coin landed on the ground. Heads appeared. Nobunaga assured them the gods had revealed their destiny to them through the coin toss, and news of their eventual victory over the enemy spread through the entire army. The soldiers continued their march towards the battleground with renewed confidence, certain that destiny couldn't be changed and they would return victorious. They fought bravely and managed to subdue their enemy while suffering very few losses on their side.

After the battle, one of the Generals approached Nobunaga. "No one could change what was destined to happen," he claimed, proudly. Nobunaga smiled and replied, "Indeed not." He then let the General in on a secret and retrieved the coin that he had used to perform the coin toss earlier. He held it up for the General, who was shocked to learn that the coin had heads on both sides.

The story illustrates how sometimes we overcomplicate matters through overthinking and end up convincing ourselves that it's impossible to overcome our problems. Whether we succeed or fail comes down to our beliefs and what we think. By changing our thinking and focusing on problem-solving instead of stressing over the problem, we can achieve a great deal more and overcome the challenges in our path. A bit of confidence and trust in our abilities to succeed goes a long way to ensure victory.

Procrastination: Entering the Maze

Procrastination is like being trapped in a maze with several passages, leading to multiple problems that could keep us stuck inside forever. Leonardo da Vinci, Samuel Johnson, Herman Melville, Bill Gates, and Steve Jobs are just some among the most famous people in history with noteworthy achievements who have also suffered the ill effects of procrastination. But in the end, they overcame their bad habit and achieved a place in history with their remarkable accomplishments.

The bestselling author of *The Handmaid's Tale*, Margaret Atwood, is a self-professed procrastinator who came up with a unique solution for her problem. She identifies different parts of her personality as two distinct people. One who is indulgent and likes to laze around and another who's rather sensible and strong-willed. Oddly enough, she named the wise and determined side of her personality "Peggy" and credits her success to Peggy's incessant nagging that finally gets her manuscript finished.

Margaret Atwood's eccentric method of kicking procrastination to the curb might not be for everyone, but it highlights the two competing sides that exist within each one of us. Our personalities can be, in fact, split into two distinct parts. One that is driven by emotions and impulses, and the other focused on doing the right thing. Bestselling author and Wharton School Professor Adam Grant agrees that Margaret's approach is backed by science. Each one of us comprises two warring sides: the *want self* and the *should self* (Stillman, 2020). When it comes to motivation, we can't rely on long-term benefits and rewards to keep us going. An alter ego like Peggy helps nudge Margaret in the right direction by reminding her of future consequences.

This is exactly the kind of force that is required to move from a state of procrastination into action. For instance, imagine that you have to write an important essay that is due in a few weeks. You experience some anxiety thinking about the essay that you keep putting off, but the level of discomfort is not enough for you to do something about it and start writing. However, a day before the deadline, the future consequence you felt you could escape becomes your present consequence. You can no longer ignore it.

The fear of failing to turn in your essay makes you jump into action and you end up completing it in a few hours. In this scenario, the pain caused by procrastinating finally escalates to unbearable levels that make you cross the "Action Line". Once you cross the action line and complete half of the essay, the pain and anxiety begin to subside. If the x-coordinate represents Time and the y-coordinate represents Pain, then the relation between time and pain would be represented by a straight line at the beginning, which rises as the time to complete the task decreases while pain increases. The peak on the graph represents the "Action Line" after which the line follows a steep decline as anxiety levels drop once we have the task underway.

The time before we reach the Action Line is far more painful than after crossing it and getting started. This shows that one of the struggles is also *getting started* on a task. Motivation and momentum gradually build up as we get our present selves to work (Clear, 2020).

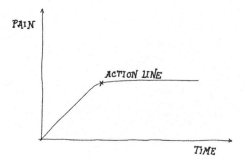

However, our willpower for getting started on a task faces certain impediments. We will now take a look at some daily enemies we come across as we try to be productive. While these factors don't necessarily make us delay getting started on a particular task, they strengthen the fears and the inhibitions mentioned in the previous chapter.

Anxiety Loops

The English psychiatrist Lionel Penrose is credited with the creation of the homonymous Penrose stairs: a set of four stairs that take 90-degree turns as they ascend or descend and make a continuous loop.

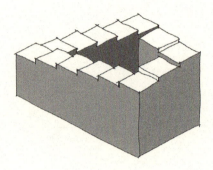

A person climbing up the stairs may keep climbing while going around in a loop, getting nowhere. Dubbed the impossible stairs, they are an excellent representation of the anxiety loop. When people get stuck, they try to manage their anxiety associated with an unpleasant task through distraction, which in turn leads to more anxiety.

On a biological level, the brains of our ancestors were designed to ensure survival by observing the surroundings to find a source of nourishment and to detect danger. The dopamine boosts that they experienced after discovering a source of food and satisfying their hunger helped them remember where they'd found it so they could return to the same place to feed themselves in the future. Human brains detect danger in a similar manner by scanning the surroundings and detecting the slightest movement to rule out the threat of attack by a vicious beast. The uncertainty helped our ancestors survive in the wild, unpredictable and hostile environment of the past.

Only when our ancestors could revisit a place again and again and be rewarded with food, without landing in unfavorable circumstances, did the uncertainty decrease. The dopamine firing occurred *in anticipation* of food to motivate our ancestors to get to the place to feed themselves.

The same process is at work when we check social media again and again, at times we need to focus our attention on an important task. Our brain has marked our Facebook and Instagram accounts as a safe place where we can find an instant dopamine boost to relax. *Distraction* is your brain relying on the old neural pathways that ensured survival for your ancestors. However, what the brain doesn't realize is that by trying to get you out of your misery, it's creating a dangerous habit. And it's pushing you towards an addictive behavior that could become hard to break.

The anxiety-distraction loop is perpetuated by a trigger-behavior-reward process we must understand if we want to break free from this vicious cycle. The process involves noticing a trigger that causes a surge of anxiety and engaging in behavior that distracts us from that anxiety, such as watching TV, eating, or playing video games. Our behavior then generates feelings of relief, which are perceived as a reward. To escape this anxiety loop, it is vital to identify our triggers and map out how the cycle plays out (Brewer, 2020).

Low Levels of Energy

While procrastination can result from feeling physically tired after a challenging day, it can also ensue from constantly putting things off. This makes us feel mentally and emotionally drained and therefore more likely to delay a task even longer. Everyone has a certain mental capacity that determines how comfortably they can handle physical and emotional distress in their lives. The nagging sense of worry of an unattended task generates mental fatigue, which can only be reduced once we finish what we started. Every time we fail to act to get a job done and off our minds, we add to our emotional load. This creates feelings of emotional fatigue, which often translate into physical exhaustion. Fatigue is self-reinforcing.

The lack of energy associated with leaving a task unfinished, or failing to begin a task, leads to more mental and emotional exhaustion, which causes us to delay even more.

Fatigue has also been linked to serious problems such as depression, sleeplessness, and lack of confidence. Think back to all those times you kept delaying a simple task. You kept telling yourself that it was a piece of cake and you'd get it done in no time. Then, once you finally got around to do it, you found yourself panicking to get it done at the eleventh hour.

By pushing seemingly simple tasks to the last minute and getting started when we're mentally and emotionally drained, we can make *simple* tasks seem more complicated than they are. It's almost as if we turn a small hill into a giant mountain in our minds through procrastination. Each time we look up at the mountain now, we feel the pull of exhaustion weighing us down as we imagine the incredible effort that it would take to climb it.

It's important to remember that just a sense of accomplishment keeps us going and gets us to finish what we started. The feeling of achievement is also self-reinforcing. The more you feel you've achieved your goals, the more motivated you feel to keep going and achieve the next goal. Since procrastination is a mood regulation mechanism, you can break the cycle of fatigue and procrastination by generating a feeling of achievement. This can be accomplished by breaking large or demanding tasks into smaller ones. Each time you reach a small milestone, you feel a rush of positive feelings which keeps you going and makes you want to achieve the next one.

Distractions

Distractions offer quick rewards and momentary relief from anxiety, but they are not the cause of procrastination. As I've mentioned many times already (and will keep doing so), the root cause of procrastination is an inability to contain fear, anxiety, and boredom that we associate with a task. They act like little allies for all the negative feelings that push us towards procrastination.

The modern digital world offers us a plethora of gadgets and gizmos to keep us connected to each other and to provide an endless stream of entertainment. From the moment we wake up, our phones and electronic devices interrupt our thought process throughout the day with the constant beeping and buzzing. It's no surprise that present generations find it harder to concentrate on a single task for long periods of time.

Psychologist Glenn Wilson, from King's College at London University, conducted 80 clinical trials on Transcutaneous Nerve Stimulation. Based on the results, he concluded that constant emails, text messages, and phone calls were a greater threat to IQ and concentration than cannabis. It was found that doziness, lethargy, and an inability to focus reached alarming levels when the respondents were bombarded with a slew of emails. The average decline of IQ was noted to be 10 points, while previous studies on cannabis found an average IQ drop of 4 points.

The impact of interruptions can be disastrous for individual productivity. A 2002 research found that most people face an interruption once every 8 minutes or 7 to 8 interruptions in an hour. On average, an interruption takes up to 5 minutes, and it takes almost 15 minutes for us to return to what we were doing and achieve the same level of concentration as before. This means that if our phone is beeping every other minute while we try to complete an important task, then we're most likely not going to concentrate and perform our best (Wainwright, 2005).

The UK's telecom regulator, Ofcom, surveyed a group of people in 2018 and reported that most check their smartphones every 12 minutes. Moreover, 71% of respondents stated that they never turn their smartphones off, while 40% said they checked their phones first thing in the morning after waking up.

Former Apple and Microsoft consultant Linda Stone, used the term Constant Partial Attention to describe recent problems with distractibility in the workplace. While distractions make us enter a constant state of alertness, they impede us from dedicating our full attention to a single task. The hormones associated with stress, adrenaline and cortisol, reach elevated levels due to frequent distractions and lack of focus. This creates a hyper-alert state in which our brains are always searching for stimuli. The brain's search for another dopamine boost makes us reach out for our smartphones again and again. We end up scrolling through social media for hours until we receive a sense of satisfaction, which gives distractibility an almost addictive quality.

Adrenaline and cortisol are meant to help us get through short bursts of activity, but over a long period, they cause the release of serotonin and dopamine, creating a sense of calm and happiness. But constant high levels of stress hormones circulating in the blood can lead to inflammation of the brain cells, making us prone to depression and anxiety. Some of us might use the word *multitasking* for the interruptions that we handle during tasks; however, a vast amount of research suggests that multitasking is a myth. You can not instantly go from dealing with a distraction to a state of full concentration, the same way that you can not fall asleep the moment your head touches the pillow.

Fragmentation of our concentration and time can easily lead to procrastination, so it's best to work on improving our focus and keeping distractions to a minimum (Griffey, 2018). In Chapter 7 I'll share my bullet-proof method that erased the word 'distraction' from my dictionary. It's so easy that it's laughable. Until you actually try it. And it'll save you hours every day. (You can also download my FREE book on Distractions, just check the QR code on page 7.)

Not Persevering

Perseverance is what keeps us going when we face obstacles in our path. It helps us regain our mental strength and keeps us focused on our end goals. But why do most of us lack perseverance and what are the ways to overcome this? Although our individual personalities play a huge role in determining how long we stay focused, perseverance is seldom considered a quality that can be attained overnight. It may take weeks or months to manage our impulses and keep ourselves focused on completing a particular task.

It's important to understand that perseverance and patience are not the same. Consistency and patience make up perseverance, so when someone perseveres, they exhibit both patience and consistency. What causes a lack of perseverance?

We want instant rewards without having to wait or work hard. Being obsessed with quick mood fixes makes it hard to keep our focus. Trying to seek instant relief makes us look for distractions that derail our focus.

We lack self-confidence and are easily discouraged. Setbacks and hardships affect our progress, and those of us who are prone to negative thoughts may lose morale and give up. The obstacles in our path can cause us to lose focus on our goal as we feel tempted to comfort ourselves in the present and find relief.

We are not consistent or patient. This could be because we are too impulsive or we simply lack patience. Other reasons for lacking consistency: a sense of distance from our future selves; discounting the value of rewards.

We may lose our motivation to complete a task after getting started because it no longer feels pleasurable. Sometimes we become distracted by new and better ideas and convince ourselves that they would yield better results. But we quickly lose interest after getting started on these new ventures and abandon them as well.

Lack of perseverance keeps us chasing after new dreams without ever reaching the finish line. It is the best recipe for living an unfulfilled life and squandering our time and resources. As I mentioned before, perseverance can't be attained overnight. It can take months of conscious thought and effort to master. However, there are several methods that can improve your focus, plowing through hardships and unfavorable circumstances to reach your goals.

Having clearly defined goals can help keep you focused as can accepting failures and mistakes. Improving your confidence and building emotional resilience can also stop you from giving in to distractions so easily (Rana, 2020).

Procrastination: A Deadly Combination of Lethargy, Interruptions, and Inconsistency

Now we know the many habits that push us towards procrastination and make it difficult for us to get started and finish tasks. Procrastination can result from a self-indulgent lifestyle where our primary focus is to seek comfort and get rid of the pain. People who frequently give in to their impulses are more likely to find a hard time staying focused. There is not a single root cause but several factors that work together to sap our motivation and fill us with negative thoughts, making us seek short-term pleasure. It takes introspection and reflection to identify the reason behind our procrastination and the factors that perpetuate it so that we can work towards eradicating it.

Key Takeaways

1. Some specific factors exacerbate procrastination: anxiety, lethargy, frequent distractions, and lack of perseverance.
2. Anxiety-distraction loops are a way for our brain to give us access to rewards and ease our present suffering. They can create patterns that mimic powerful addictions and can be notoriously difficult to break.

3. Lack of energy can be a cause of procrastination: constantly putting off a task depletes our mental capacity and leaves us feeling emotionally and mentally exhausted, which leads to more procrastination.
4. Distractions are impossible to avoid in today's digital world. They affect productivity and performance, as it takes a long time to build the same level of concentration once we're interrupted.
5. Lack of perseverance is caused by a deficiency of patience and consistency. We're more likely to stop working on a task once it stops giving us the same feelings of excitement and pleasure that it did in the beginning.
6. Self-awareness is key for breaking out of these addictive patterns. We need to identify our triggers and the methods we use to soothe ourselves in times of distress. And eventually replace them with less harmful behavior, to avoid getting trapped in these cycles again and again.

PART 3: CONQUER THE ENEMY

CHAPTER FIVE: HOW TO FINISH WHAT YOU STARTED

"A dream written down with a date becomes a goal. A goal broken down into steps becomes a plan. A plan backed by action makes your dreams come true."

— Greg S. Reid

Now that we know why we keep putting off important tasks for later, let's look at ways to beat this malicious habit. The goal is to pick up where we left off and finish what we started. If you've let things pile up until they're stacked as high as the ceiling, it's virtually impossible to get anything done on time. If you are in that position, then it's time to re-evaluate your life and figure out where you went wrong.

As we discussed in previous chapters, there are different types of procrastination and different reasons that cause people to delay action. These are based on people's unique personalities, which means there can't be a unique solution to procrastination for everyone. There is no "one size fits all" fix that most websites and blogs would have you believe. To beat the enemy, you must identify your triggers and analyze your behavior so that you can find the right solution for yourself. In this chapter, I'm going to help you do just that by showing different ways to keep your delaying tactics at bay and stay focused on the goal.

Let's get started on our journey by looking at ways of minimizing procrastination and building the resolve to change ourselves.

Improving Our Emotional Regulation Skills

By now, we've established that procrastination *is not* something that just happens because you're bad at time management. *It is* a way for you to cope with difficult emotions. So, to kick the habit of dilly dallying to the curb, you first need to learn to control your emotions. There are two ways to achieve emotional regulation: adaptive and maladaptive.

Adaptive Emotion Regulation

Adaptive strategies for emotion regulation allow you to cope with unpleasant situations in positive ways. These strategies are based on the following factors:

Acceptance
Positive refocusing
Focusing on planning
Putting things into perspective
Positive reappraisals

Acceptance involves being honest with yourself about your feelings. Let's say you have to complete a task that you don't like. You can either let the negative emotions overwhelm you and try to handle the difficult feelings by avoiding the task. Or you can accept the feelings and let them run their course.

Positive refocusing involves directing your focus on those aspects of the tasks that you do enjoy instead of fixating on what makes the task difficult and unpleasant.

Focusing on planning means thinking about the actions that you can take to minimize your distress and ease your anxiety. If you are working on a big assignment, then thinking about ways to make it more manageable is going to increase your productivity rather than pondering over the complicated nature and level of difficulty of the assignment.

Putting things into perspective means accepting that the negative feelings have passed and you don't need to stay stuck thinking about your negative emotions.

Positive reappraisals means trying to find something positive in a negative experience. Maybe the task that's been filling you with dread could help to improve your skills or increase your knowledge. When you focus on what makes an activity important, then it becomes much easier to sacrifice short-term pleasure for hard work that would yield much bigger gains in the future.

Overall, adaptive strategies for emotion regulation focus on acceptance of one's negative emotions: finding practical ways to minimize our discomfort while staying focused on the finish line.

Maladaptive Emotion Regulation

Maladaptive strategies for emotion regulation revolve around amplifying our negative emotions by constantly thinking about the negative aspects of a task and delaying it to gain short-term relief. They are based on:

- Self-blame
- Rumination
- Catastrophizing
- Blaming others

Self-blame and rumination involve blaming oneself for the negative emotions and thinking about the discomfort associated with the activity at hand.

Catastrophizing is imagining how awful it would be for us to attempt the task and imagining terrible consequences for ourselves if we fail to complete it on time.

Blaming others involves refusing to take responsibility for our actions. While we may castigate and chide ourselves for not getting a task done, we might also extend the blame to other people or to our circumstances, finding comfort in the thought that procrastination was unavoidable (Domaradzka & Fajkowska, 2018).

Maladaptive strategies for emotion regulation focus on avoiding negative emotions by engaging in other activities. Exacerbating negative thoughts related to a task through self-flagellation. By avoiding maladaptive strategies and adopting *adaptive strategies* to cope with negative emotions, we can effectively tackle procrastination. Adaptive strategies can help us deal with frustration and anger positively by acknowledging our negative emotions and focusing on problem-solving rather than avoiding uncomfortable feelings by denying their presence (Eckert et al., 2016).

Forgive Yourself

Can getting rid of procrastination be as easy as forgiving yourself for dilly dallying in the past? The results of a 2010 study on 119 University students give compelling evidence that the simple act of forgiving yourself for procrastinating in the past could help you avoid procrastination in the future. The study found that students who practiced self-forgiveness for procrastinating on the previous exam were less likely to put off studying for the next one (Wohl et al., 2010).

It may seem deceivingly simple, but there is a catch. Forgiving yourself doesn't mean overlooking procrastination while it happens. Such a mindset can lead to complacency and having very low standards for yourself. The trick is to not let past guilt overcome you and impede your current progress.

Change the Way You Look at Relapses

Once we make up our mind about getting rid of procrastination, it can be frustrating to see ourselves slipping back into old habits. The more we try to fight these relapses, the more difficult it may seem to stick to our new resolution and stay focused. We may end up believing that it's impossible to beat procrastination. That we are doomed to spend the rest of our life frantically trying to get things done at the last minute and scraping through.

What we don't realize is that relapses are common and completely natural. The occasional relapse you might experience is only a small part of a much longer journey. Don't let minor bumps in the road derail your progress. Researchers James Prochaska and Carlo DiClemente introduced the stages of change in the late 1970s while studying ways to help people stop smoking:

Precontemplation
Contemplation

Preparation
Action
Maintenance
Relapse

If we take the example of someone who wants to quit eating junk food and start eating healthy, then the first stage of their journey would be marked by denial or ignorance. During precontemplation, individuals resign to their current circumstances and develop the erroneous belief that they have no control over their behavior. For example, a person who has a junk food addiction may go on ignoring his or her doctor's advice and continue with unhealthy eating habits. A small dose of self-awareness can push us in the right direction and motivate us to change our self-harming behaviors. Analyzing our actions and assessing the risks associated with our current behavior can nudge us toward the next stage: contemplation.

In this stage, people become more aware of the potential benefits of changing their behaviors; yet, the price they have to pay to achieve this change makes them reconsider.

The third stage is characterized by an internal conflict between seeking short-term pleasure or persevering for long-term gains. The tug-of-war between impulses and long-term benefits makes people ambivalent about committing to change. Many individuals fail to make it past this stage. However, overcoming this phase leads to preparation and action in which people finally take charge of their circumstances and come up with a plan to get themselves out of their current predicament.

The fifth stage, maintenance, involves sticking to new habits and resisting the temptation to return to old behaviors. The longer we are able to maintain our new behaviors, the more self-assured we become in our ability to continue the change.

Finally, the last stage, relapse, is characterized by disappointment, feelings of failure, and frustration, but is a common occurrence. Using this stage to identify triggers, pinpoints the barrier to success. Refocusing on our goal can help us overcome this stage and continue changing our behaviors.

Ever gone on a strict diet and lost your motivation after giving in to one donut? Ever committed yourself to cleaning the house only to give up a few hours later after a short break turns into a TV marathon? You don't know what happened. You ignore how you ended up watching the first 5 episodes of a new TV series, but there's no point in quitting now: you must find out how it ends. Cleaning can wait.

Relapses can be difficult and they can chip away our motivation to continue changing ourselves for the better. But they open a window into our unique psyche. If we spend some time asking ourselves difficult questions about why we keep succumbing to temptations, we could uncover our weaknesses and put ourselves in a better position to succeed later on.

Relapse could either cause us to quit attempting to change ourselves. Or it could bring us back to preparation, action, and maintenance armed with new information we can use to troubleshoot problems and come up with a better plan to help us succeed (Cherry,

2021). So, while you should try to resist relapses as much as possible, it is also important to minimize the negative impact of an occasional relapse. Use it to propel forward instead of letting it hold you back. In 2009, Phillipa Lally and her research team studied habit formation among 96 volunteers. The participants chose an eating, drinking, or activity behavior they had to carry out daily for 13 weeks. Results showed how missing one opportunity to perform the behavior did not affect the habit formation process.

Our attitude toward a relapse, whether we deal with minor regressions in a positive or negative way, determines our success or failure to continue improving our behavior. A negative way to deal with a relapse we should avoid is accepting our inability to complete a task, believing we would never get it done. If you end up stuffing one donut, you might convince yourself that it's okay to give up on your diet altogether and eat a few more since you've already messed up.

If you end up relapsing, here are a few steps you should follow to minimize its impact:

The sooner you become honest with yourself and accept that you've been delaying action, the better it is for you to repair the damage. Living in denial and refusing to take responsibility for your actions only worsens the impact of procrastination.

Once you come to terms that you've relapsed, don't let the guilt stop you from taking action to fix your mistake. Instead of beating yourself up over what has happened, you can focus your energy on the steps you can take to get yourself back on track.

Focus on problem-solving rather than regretting your mistakes. Try to look at the situation from different viewpoints and brainstorm ideas to figure out why you keep procrastinating.

Once you complete what you had to, you can go over the entire incident. Note down what you can learn from the experience so that you don't relapse again in the future.

Build Self-Compassion
Self-compassion encourages adaptive emotion-regulation strategies which reduce the chances you'll procrastinate again in the future. Delaying a task as a way to deal with negative emotions only makes it more difficult for you to concentrate on what you're doing.

Professor Fuschia Sirois and her team studied the effect of self-compassion on bedtime procrastination. They found that self-compassionate people were less likely to procrastinate because of cognitive reappraisal, which helps in negative mood repair. Cognitive reappraisal can be defined as an attempt to reinterpret an emotional situation in a way that changes its meaning and impact (Cutuli, 2014). Researchers found that self-compassionate people reported higher levels of positive feelings and engaged in less bedtime procrastination.

Most of us see harsh self-criticism as a motivating factor. However, science tells us that this is most likely not true. Beating ourselves up for procrastinating only increases the likelihood that we'd engage in the same delaying tactics again in the future. Self-compassion helps you extend sympathy to yourself when you're feeling terrible about your past mistakes. It minimizes stress and helps you deal with the negative emotions ensuing from procrastination. Self-compassion comprises the following factors:

Self-kindness: The ability to treat yourself with kindness instead of being critical of yourself for falling short of your expectations.

Humanity: Self-compassion allows you to extend kindness, compassion, and understanding to other people around you. It changes your perspective on imperfection. You begin seeing it as a shared human experience rather than something that isolates one person from everyone else.

Mindfulness: Being kind to ourselves helps us develop mindfulness, which is the ability to experience the present moment and accept our thoughts and feelings without judgment. Through mindfulness, we can live in the moment without letting negative emotions overwhelm us.

Self-criticism leads to self-handicapping, which is a type of self-sabotage. We avoid putting in our best effort in order to protect our ego. A leading researcher in the field of studying procrastination, Kristin Neff, writes in her book *Self-Compassion*: "*Research indicates that self-critics are less likely to achieve their goals because of these sorts of self-handicapping strategies. In one study, for instance, college students were asked to describe their various academic, social, and health-related goals, and then to report on how much progress they had made toward these goals. Self-critics made significantly less progress toward their goals than others and also reported that they procrastinate more often."*

Self-sabotage includes passing up on a job opportunity because you think you wouldn't make it. Or not studying for an exam, so you can blame your poor grades on lack of preparation rather than having people think you're not intelligent enough. You may beat yourself up later hoping the incident doesn't repeat itself, but negative self-talk will most likely trigger more self-defeating behavior in the future.

Think about it, you turn toward procrastination to deal with negative emotional states. Self-criticism may force you to get you off the couch and get some of the work done, but negative self-talk is bound to make you feel bad in the long run. This means you will eventually turn back to the same coping skills that helped you deal with negative emotions before and find yourself procrastinating again.

While self-criticism comes naturally to most of us, it's difficult to develop self-compassion. Here are some techniques you can employ to develop a habit of treating yourself with kindness (Harvard Health Publishing, 2021):

Practice mindfulness: Spending a few minutes meditating can help you connect with the present moment and accept your negative feelings.

Encouragement: While most of us don't find it hard to be kind to others, we feel awkward when we need to offer words of encouragement to ourselves. Befriend yourself and offer words of encouragement when you're feeling low.

Relax your body: Take a few minutes' breaks from whatever you're doing and try to relax. Sit in a quiet place for a few minutes and take a few deep breaths.

When we find ourselves in a difficult situation, we must offer ourselves encouragement and stay in the moment. Being kind to ourselves may feel unnatural at first, but it helps reduce negative emotions and cope with hard feelings constructively. A great way to remind yourself to practice self-kindness is to think about how you would treat a friend in trouble. While self-compassion is essential in helping us cope with negative emotions, it's important that we make sure it doesn't lead to more delaying.

Often, we confuse self-compassion with complacency and end up procrastinating even more. So when you're practicing kindness toward yourself, ask yourself whether it is helping you stay focused or it's making you lower your standards and procrastinate more.

Becoming Self-Organized

We've established throughout this book that procrastination is not a time-management problem, but a failure to regulate our moods and emotions. While that is true, a certain level of organization is still necessary to beat it. Here are some strategies that will drastically improve your chances of finishing what you started.

1 - Set SMART Goals
Setting SMART goals can make a difference in making sure you get things done. In my early twenties, when I was struggling with a bad case of feeling low on motivation, I had little to no idea about what I wanted to do with my future, which was one reason I didn't feel motivated to do anything about it. A training workshop at my old job introduced me to the idea of SMART goals. I remember the light bulb moment I had while sitting in the audience. I had never stopped to ask myself the big questions. This was why my hopes and dreams never felt important to me and I never put in a good amount of effort to achieve them.

SMART is an acronym for Specific, Measurable, Achievable, Relevant, and Time-bound.

"I want to get fit" is a great goal to have, but it's missing crucial details such as *why, when, and how*. We are more likely to achieve a goal that carries meaning than a vague one. The first step of setting SMART goals is to ask ourselves why we want to achieve it. If you're working on an assignment, then ask yourself *why* it matters that you complete it? Would it increase your chances of getting promoted? Or would it help you get a better grade? What makes this assignment meaningful to you?

Once you've answered the above questions, you can move on and settle on a way to track your progress. For example, if your goal is to study for an exam, then you can break the topics that you have to prepare into smaller milestones you need to achieve in a defined time frame. For instance, you set a daily target of reading ten pages or completing one chapter in two days. These small milestones could lead up to a bigger goal, like finishing your studies a few days before the exam.

It's also necessary to make sure that we set achievable goals for ourselves. Deciding to cram everything a night before the exam is most likely setting yourself up for failure. Whatever your goal is, it should have meaning in your life and align with your purpose. If you consider a task or a project irrelevant to what you believe in, then chances are you'd have a hard time seeing it through.

Finally, the most important part of the goal-setting process is deciding on a time frame to get things done. Attaching a goal to a deadline creates a sense of urgency and gives you a sense of direction. Using the techniques given above, the goal "I want to get fit" would look something like "I want to lose 10 pounds by December because I want to feel healthy and strong." If you have to write an academic essay, then you can start earlier and set a daily target of writing 500 words, which is way more achievable than trying to churn out 10,000 words a day.

2 - Identifying the Problem

Without understanding exactly where you're going wrong, you won't know where to start. You need to find out exactly why you keep running around in circles, delaying important tasks repeatedly. There are three factors that determine the exact nature of your procrastination:

Finding yourself in certain situations may cause you to procrastinate more than others. When are you most likely to postpone what you should actually do? For example, is it easier to delay tasks when you're working from home than when you have to work at your office?

What activities do you engage in when you're procrastinating? Do you frequently end up scrolling through social media when you need to focus your attention on completing an important task? Or do you spend hours browsing the web? How you choose to procrastinate can help you identify specific patterns that you need to change by replacing them with healthier and calming alternatives.

What causes you to procrastinate? This is the most important question that you need to answer to get to the root of the problem. Exactly what makes you put things off for later? Is it because you're easily distracted or because you feel overwhelmed?

Here's how you can use the three questions above to find out the root cause of your procrastination. If you have to work on a university project but you keep delaying it, then you could use those questions to figure out the exact source for your lack of motivation. You might not feel motivated enough to work on the project while you're at home and feel tempted to play video games instead because you think it is too boring.

You could tackle this problem by breaking down the project into smaller parts and deciding on a time and place to work on them that offers minimal distractions. You can spark your interest in the project by focusing on the parts that you find interesting. The reason we procrastinate includes the following factors:

An inflated sense of confidence in our own abilities to complete a task in the shortest amount of time. How many times have you procrastinated thinking to yourself that it'd take you a mere few minutes to get the job done? I know I have put things off for later far too many times because of the false sense of security that unrealistic confidence in my own abilities creates. If you find yourself unbothered by a task that you've left unattended, try asking yourself if it's really possible to get it done in the time you *think* it would take to get it finished. And if the task is so easy, then why not start working on it sooner than later so that you can get it out of the way.

Feeling disconnected from our future selves or focusing too much on future possibilities. When you say that your future self would get the work done in record time, are you sure that you're talking about yourself? The reason you have so much faith in your future self's abilities could be because you feel you won't have to bear the brunt of your poor decisions. Maybe you don't identify with the person who would hand in the assignment late.

Feeling overwhelmed, anxious, fearful, lacking motivation, and striving for perfectionism could all contribute to your procrastination. These are factors we've discussed in detail in Chapter 3. Revisit that chapter to figure out exactly what kind of procrastination you are suffering from.

3 - Develop A Plan of Action

There's not much that you can achieve without a plan of action. Identifying your triggers that derail your focus can help you come up with a plan for damage control. This is a roadmap that will help you navigate through difficult emotional states without succumbing to procrastination. To develop a plan of action, you need to know which method works best for you. There are two kinds of techniques that can be employed to reign in procrastination:

Behavioral techniques: These techniques involve directly correcting your behavior and trying to adopt positive habits. Some examples of positive behaviors to minimize procrastination include: getting rid of distractions or breaking an enormous task into smaller, more manageable tasks.

Cognitive techniques: Cognitive techniques are based on changing your thought patterns and instilling positive thoughts in place of negative ones. Some techniques to achieve mental fortitude and resist procrastination include: focusing on rewards, connecting with your future selves, and visualizing yourself succeeding.

You can use a combination of both cognitive and behavioral methods to overcome procrastination. In order to stop yourself from putting things off for later, you need to replace negative thoughts and behaviors with positive ones. Of course, this is easier said than done, but you're more likely to achieve some level of improvement once you commit to changing yourself. Remember, the first step in solving a problem is self-awareness. You've already achieved that by recognizing the type of procrastination you usually engage in, identifying your triggers, and pinpointing the reasons you find it so tempting to keep postponing what you have to do. Some simple ways to use these techniques include:

If you're working on a document late at night, then you can try leaving it open on your computer so that you can pick up where you left off the next morning. Similarly, if you're writing a report or an essay, you can leave it open on your bedside when you go to sleep so that you feel motivated to finish the rest of it in the morning.

Get rid of distractions. Put your phone on silent mode, have your video games out of sight, turn off email notifications, and log out of your social media accounts while you sit down to complete a task. The more you're able to keep yourself focused, the easier it'll be for you to complete the task on time.

Replace negative behaviors with positive ones. If you feel a strong urge to stop working and find mental or emotional relief by playing video games or using social media, then try taking a quick break and go for a brisk walk instead. Light physical exercise will make you feel more alert and motivated to get back to the task and finish it, making it a much better alternative to video games or social media, which are engineered to be addictive and difficult to quit.

Finding the right technique for you to overcome procrastination involves trial and error. What works for one person may not work for another. You may feel disappointed when, despite your best efforts to change yourself, you continue leaving things for the last minute. During such times, it's important to remember that even a single step counts as progress and it's better than taking no action at all.

Key Takeaways

1. Improve your emotional regulation skills and try to develop adaptive emotional regulation rather than maladaptive practices.
2. Learn to forgive yourself, build self-compassion, and change the way you perceive mistakes.
3. Become organized by setting SMART goals, identifying triggers, and using cognitive and behavioral techniques to make a plan of action.

CHAPTER SIX: SOLUTIONS FOR DIFFERENT TYPES OF PROCRASTINATORS

"We all sorely complain of the shortness of time, and yet have much more than we know what to do with. Our lives are either spent in doing nothing at all, or in doing nothing to the purpose, or in doing nothing that we ought to do. We are always complaining that our days are few, and acting as though there would be no end of them."

— Seneca

You have to find a solution that matches your type. There is no single answer to solve procrastination for everyone. This is why soul-searching is essential to find the correct fix for your delaying habit.

Type 1: Self Deception and Planning Failures

Is your procrastination a result of a false sense of security? Maybe you keep putting things off because you think it wouldn't take you so long to finish it in the future, or maybe you convince yourself that the consequences of not getting it finished wouldn't be so bad. If you keep falling for procrastination time and again and don't know how to escape this vicious cycle, here are the solutions that will yield the best results.

Break Big Tasks into Smaller Tasks
Aside from *finishing what we started*, you might also find it hard to get started on a project or activity. Especially when the workload is massive, it's easy to feel overwhelmed. Hence, dividing a complicated or big task into smaller ones will make it seem less daunting and motivate you to get started.

As you achieve smaller milestones, you'll feel a sense of accomplishment that will keep you motivated until the end. You can reward yourself for making progress, to keep you going until you finish the entire task. Simplifying a project in this way also helps you plan. The short milestones create a roadmap that leads you, so you always know where you're going.

If you have to write a report, then you can divide it into different subtasks, such as gathering the data, writing the introduction, and writing the middle and conclusion. Here are a few things to keep in mind when you follow these techniques:

You don't need to have the entire project outlined down to every minute detail from start to finish. Stressing about having it all planned out can become an excuse for more delay.

Focus on taking small first steps to get yourself going. It can be as simple as taking a few minutes to jot down a few points about the introduction or reading the first few paragraphs.

You can break subtasks into even smaller tasks to make the job simpler, manageable, and encourage yourself to keep moving forward.

Learn to Prioritize

Decide which tasks are important (that you need to finish first) and which you can leave for later. By prioritizing tasks based on their significance, you can avoid wasting time on unimportant tasks and use your energy and time to complete the things that matter most. This also helps get rid of the overwhelming feeling of not knowing where to start. However, you may face some difficulty deciding which tasks to consider essential or non-essential. This can sometimes lead to decision fatigue when we waste valuable time trying to decide what to do. Enter the Ivy Lee Method and the Eisenhower Matrix.

The Ivy Lee Method

This method involves taking a few minutes every night to jot down 5 to 6 important tasks that you have to get done the next day. This technique minimizes decision fatigue as you prioritize tasks based on their level of difficulty. You start off by doing the most complicated task first and move down the list until you've finished the six tasks that you decided the night before. Any task that is left uncompleted is added to the to-do list of the next day.

Eisenhower Matrix

This is an excellent method for time management and involves organizing tasks based on their importance and urgency. The Eisenhower matrix comprises four categories. The first category is for tasks that are both urgent and important, so they can't be delayed. The second includes tasks that are not urgent but important, such as exercising or taking a break from work when you're mentally exhausted. The third category consists of tasks that are urgent but not important, such as answering a phone call or replying to non-essential emails. The fourth and last includes activities that are neither important nor urgent, such as watching a TV series or playing video games.

So, how should you approach the activities you've categorized?

	URGENT	NOT URGENT
IMPORTANT	DO (Important + Urgent)	DECIDE (Important + Not Urgent)
NOT IMPORTANT	DELEGATE (Important + Not Urgent)	ELIMINATE (Not Important + Not Urgent)

Do what is in the first category.

Decide on when to deal with tasks in the second category.

Delegate tasks in the third category.

Eliminate what's in the fourth category.

Do not spend too much time trying to get things in order and delaying actual work on an assignment. Keep things simple and avoid overcomplicating everything. Remember that sorting tasks based on importance and urgency is only to speed up progress. If you find yourself feeling overwhelmed or confused about the organization aspect, then it's best to use the Ivy Lee method to settle on a few important tasks and get yourself started.

Reduce the Number of Decisions You Have to Make

Minimizing the number of decisions you have to make can also reduce decision fatigue to get you quickly started on a task.

Choosing your clothes the night before can help you avoid the stress of choosing what to wear in the morning. Similarly, deciding on which part of an assignment you need to do first well before you get started can help save time.

If you struggle with decision making and end up prolonging the process, then you should put a time limit on it. You can use a timer and settle on a decision once the time's up. This can help you avoid fretting over getting everything right, which is another way to make sure you don't spend too much time racking your brain trying to find the right way to go about doing something.

Get Rid of Bottlenecks

Sometimes the reason we keep procrastinating is that we can't get an important task completed and we can't move on to the next ones. Such tasks act as a bottleneck, stopping us from crossing off the other items on our to-do list. Here are some ways to address bottlenecks:

If the task is complex and time-consuming, then you can postpone it for a little while and get other things done so that you start feeling a sense of accomplishment. Reward yourself by crossing off other important items on your list so that you return to address the first task with renewed vigor.

Try modifying the task to make it simpler. If you're writing a report and find yourself stuck on a specific part, then ask yourself whether the information is essential or not. Use a different method or try a different approach to overcome the impasse.

If, no matter what you do, you're unable to get the task done, if you have the option, hand it over to someone else or ask for someone to help you. Sometimes we come to realize that the task that had been holding us back from moving on isn't as important as we thought it was, so it's best to eliminate it entirely.

Like everything else, the most important thing is to first identify what we're dealing with: a bottleneck. Then, we can try different techniques to work around it. Different methods work for different people. The success of a technique depends on an individual's personality and the nature and complexity of the task at hand.

Type 2: Fears and Insecurities

If insecurities such as low self-esteem, fear of failure, or perfectionism are holding you back, then you need to work on defeating your inner demons first.

Know Your Fears
Being honest with ourselves about exactly what we're afraid of can help us get over our fears by thinking of ways to tackle them.

Sometimes the reason behind our procrastination is simply that we're not addressing our fears. We're avoiding them instead.

Years ago, I remember putting off an assignment for days, because it involved public speaking. I put it on the back burner and forgot all about it for the first few weeks. Then, I finally found the motivation to get working on the task once I came to terms with my fear of public speaking. I focused on the research and on writing parts of the assignment, *purposefully ignoring the presentation.* Why? I realized I needed excellent material to feel confident to give a good presentation. I still needed to practice my public speaking skills, but I knew that could wait while I concentrated on getting the written material ready.

By accepting my fear, I was able to push it aside for a while instead of getting paralyzed by it, so that I could complete the task at hand. I put my best effort into creating a kick-ass presentation and, because I felt happy with my work, I found the confidence to stand in front of the class and give my presentation. Let's be clear, it wasn't a TED Talk, but I still got a genuine applause at the end.

Avoid Perfectionism

So many of us get stuck trying to achieve perfection. You may start an essay or a report and get as far as writing a few sentences before crumpling the paper in your hands and tossing it in the trash can. Perfectionism often pushes us toward procrastination and breeds dissatisfaction with our work, no matter how hard we try. Here are some ways a quest for perfection can impede your progress:

The pressure of doing a task perfectly can make you delay getting started. You may feel an overwhelming sense of fear (and stress) that you won't be able to execute it perfectly and decide to avoid it altogether.

It can cause you to keep revising your work continuously, because you never consider it good enough. You may start over again and again as you struggle to meet your own lofty standards.

Usually perfectionism and fear of criticism go hand-in-hand, so you may struggle to show your work to others. It may stop you from publishing a book or displaying your artwork. You may find yourself paralyzed and stuck in one place.

While it's alright to use all the resources available and try to come up with the best ways to complete a project, be mindful. If the preparation, or simply writing the introduction, takes too long, then you're probably stuck trying to achieve the unachievable. At its essence, perfectionism is fueled by low self-esteem and a lack of confidence. It's when we are riddled with so many self-doubts that cripple our progress and keep us stranded. It is helpful to accept that no one is perfect and that it's near impossible to attain perfection. All we can do is put in our best efforts, learn from our mistakes and improve ourselves.

Increase Your Self-Efficacy and Build a Positive Outlook

Self-efficacy is the belief in our ability to overcome unforeseen obstacles and problems that may come our way. Possessing a healthy level of self-efficacy is crucial for achieving self-regulation. This helps us beat procrastination and get started on what we deem unpleasant or frightening. A study published in *Contemporary Educational Psychology* examined a group of undergraduates to find a relation between procrastination, self-regulation, and self-efficacy. Of the 195 participants in the study, 25% were classified as procrastinators and displayed low self-efficacy and self-regulation (Klassen et al., 2008).

Moreover, self-efficacy has been linked to being hopeful. A 2007 study examined the connection between hope and procrastination by analyzing the responses of 116 university students to the Procrastination Assessment Scale for Students (PASS) and the Adult Hope Scale. The results suggest that a lack of hope was an accurate prediction of academic procrastination. Feeling hopeful or optimistic about the future could minimize procrastination (Alexander & Onwuegbuzie, 2007). So, how can you stop imagining the worst possible outcomes and build a positive mindset? There are two ways of thinking that can inspire hope:

Pathway Thinking: We think about different ways to overcome an obstacle and solve a problem. Our minds explore different options as we strategize and plan to work our way around hurdles, trying to achieve our goals. Pathway thinking helps us to focus on the things we can do and that are within our control.

Agency Thinking: This includes the belief that we are capable of working toward our goals, achieving success. It gives us the motivation to pursue our objectives and overcome obstacles. These thoughts include how competent we consider ourselves, the belief in our abilities, and readiness for action.

We can increase hopefulness by thinking about past victories and visualizing success. However, it's crucial we don't get too carried away with our optimism about the future and lower our expectations in the process. An unrealistic amount of positivity or overconfidence in our abilities to get a task done can lead to more procrastination. So, while we should adopt a more positive outlook, we must remain level-headed and avoid getting too comfortable.

Surround Yourself with Supportive People
Surround yourself with people who are motivated and hardworking, so that you too feel motivated to get things done. If you're hanging out with individuals who're rarely ever bothered about approaching deadlines and enjoy spending their time on Netflix instead, then you'd most likely do the same. As the motivational speaker Jim Rohn famously said, *we are the average of the five people we spend the most time with*. There are two key aspects you should think about when you build new friendships:

Seek Positive Peer Influence
Surround yourself with people who're goal-oriented, work hard, hold themselves accountable, stay focused, and encourage others to do the

same. People who have these attributes are going to have a good influence on you and push you to be the best.

Avoid Negative Peer Influence
Now, you don't have to go around breaking friendships in a dramatic fashion just so you can get your assignment finished on time. It is, however, important that you analyze your relationships and decide whether you've been giving in to peer pressure lately and procrastinating as a result. If your friends always end up convincing you to go out with them when you really should concentrate on your work, then it's time to start standing up for yourself. Limit the time you spend with people who are constantly indulging in short-term pleasures and pay little to no attention to important tasks.

Ask for Help
If you're stuck, then it's okay to ask for help. You may find it easier to beat procrastination if you're able to vent your frustration to someone and have them cheer you on. You can either ask them to help you with a project or ask them to help you stay focused. Team up with someone who is highly motivated to keep you on track and help you get over procrastination. An additional tip: if you're going to vent your frustration to a friend, make sure you put a time limit first. If you spend over 15 minutes talking about your procrastination, then you're actually procrastinating.

Type 3: Lack of Motivation

If you belong to Type 3, you procrastinate because you feel drained and unmotivated. You can't seem to find your spark and feel no desire to achieve your goals. If ennui and boredom are holding you back, then the following *solutions* will get back to work.

The Importance of Deadlines
Deadlines are a great way to create a sense of urgency. They can be used strategically to motivate yourself to complete small milestones and to keep you committed. You can allow yourself small rewards as you complete each target. However, there are a few things you should consider before you decide on a deadline.

Set concrete and specific deadlines rather than vague ones. For example, "I'll get the job done next week" won't be as effective in keeping you motivated as "I will get the job done by 5pm on Wednesday."

Be realistic and don't set a deadline that is impossible for you to achieve. Avoid overestimating your capabilities and allow yourself enough time to complete a task without feeling stressed or pressured. Again, be honest with yourself about how much work you can handle and how quickly you can get it done. Set deadlines that are meaningful. Deadlines are useful as long as you respect them and abide by them. If you feel no qualms over breaking deadlines, then there's really no point in setting a time limit to get things done.

Setting deadlines should motivate you to start on a project sooner than later. If you are setting a deadline that's too distant in the future, then you may not feel the urgency or slight pressure to get the job done. This is why it is important to set small deadlines that match with each milestone so you can keep track of your progress instead of having just a single deadline to complete the entire task.

Dividing an enormous task into smaller chunks helps us set the deadlines that are near in the future. This makes it more likely that we'll take them seriously. Self-imposed deadlines are also useful when you don't have a clearly defined or external deadline. This is usually the case for goals related to personal development, such as losing weight, becoming more confident, or starting a new business.

Reward Yourself for Your Achievements

We're usually extremely hard on ourselves when we fail, but ignore happiness when we accomplish something. It's important that we celebrate small wins and appreciate our effort to keep us moving forward. Short-term rewards that are associated with hard work can help reduce chances of procrastination in the future and avoid mental and emotional fatigue, which may ensue if you're stuck doing a boring job for too long.

You can reward yourself when you complete a milestone by reading a book or taking a walk around the block. However, it is best to avoid activities engineered to become addictive like video games or watching a TV series. You can create a sense of accomplishment in simpler ways by crossing off the items on your to-do list or writing down the number of tasks that you've completed.

Don't Lose Sight of the Goal

Keep your eyes on the prize and stay focused on the end goal instead of letting the unpleasantness of the activity at hand overwhelm you. If you can't seem to complete it because you find it boring, then focus on the goal you're working toward. Try to visualize yourself making it to the finish line and succeeding at what you set out to do.

This approach is known as *outcome focus*, and it is most beneficial when procrastination stems from task aversion. In some cases, when we fear the consequences of turning in our work or finishing a task, it is better to remain *process focused* to reduce the fear of failure or criticism that may paralyze us.

Visualize Yourself Succeeding

Visualizing your future self completing a task and gaining rewards is crucial to keeping motivation high. **You can overcome procrastination through a technique called *episodic future thinking*, the ability to imagine experiences in the future.**

This technique helps us connect with our future selves and creates a sense of responsibility by making us realize we will be the ones who'd bear the consequences of our actions. Try to be as vivid and detailed during visualization as possible so that you feel the positive or negative emotions your future self will experience. The better you can imagine accurately how things will play out in the future, the more you will feel connected with your future self and care about what happens to you in the months and years to come. This technique changed my life. From getting my master's degree, to writing this book, this is my 'go-to' hack to making sure I accomplish my long-term goals. In Chapter 7 you'll learn exactly how I use it.

Bonus Weapons for Beating Procrastination

Now that we've covered the basis, here I've outlined further techniques and strategies that can skyrocket your productivity, making you unstoppable.

Find Out Your Productivity Cycle

A large part of getting over a bad habit involves self-analysis. Becoming aware of the patterns you follow, your preferences, and your pet peeves lets you build a clear picture of where you stand, how you can overcome your problems, and map out your future. Pay close attention to your performance throughout the day to figure out when you're the most productive, the time of the day when you can get the most work done. Some people perform well in the morning right after a strong cup of coffee, while others are able to accomplish the most later on in the day.

Track your cycle of productivity and figure out the highs and lows. You can use this information to schedule the most important tasks when your energy and motivation are at their peak and avoid working during the times your energy slumps.

Build a Routine

You can keep yourself motivated for longer if you follow a routine instead of picking and dismissing tasks on a whim throughout the day. Fix a time for your work and avoid assignments from spilling into the hours when you need to rest. Setting up a routine can stop you from working late at night, messing up your sleep pattern.

Get Yourself Immersed in the Task

In the previous chapters, I mentioned the Action Line and how procrastination keeps us from reaching it. However, it gets easier to complete a task once we get over our initial hesitation and get started. When you start working, a time comes when you become so immersed in what you're doing that you forget everything else and thoroughly enjoy the work at hand. This is known as the *flow state*, when it's hard to break your concentration as you remain focused on what you're doing and draw pleasure and satisfaction by engaging in the work. You can push yourself to achieve the flow state by choosing a quiet place with no distractions and working when you are most productive.

Plan for the Future

If you're prone to postpone tasks, then it's best to prepare in advance and have a contingency plan ready. One reason people fail to beat procrastination is that despite their best intentions, they cannot plan ahead. You can minimize the chances of future procrastination by identifying scenarios where you may have trouble self-regulating your emotions. You can recognize your triggers to anticipate *when* you might procrastinate and replace the behaviors you usually engage in to seek short-term relief with more productive ones.

Boost Your Energy Levels

Yes, this sounds like the simplest suggestion ever. Yet, most people often look for advanced solutions instead of making sure the basics are covered. Take care of your health to keep your energy up so that you can handle most activities with ease. Make sure that you clock up on sleep, eat well and drink plenty of water. Exercise regularly to keep your mind and body healthy. You can hit the gym to lift weights or run on a treadmill or keep it simple, like going for a walk around the block. Regular exercise also helps keep stress levels down. Since we know that stress can exacerbate procrastination, it's best to burn those calories by keeping it moving.

Delay Short-Term Relief

If you're finding it hard to resist temptation, then try delaying the gratification process. If you feel an overwhelming urge to pick up your phone and scroll through Facebook, then try waiting for 10 or 20 seconds to see if the impulse passes. Usually, an urge to engage in old habits doesn't last for too long. If you're able to delay giving in to the impulse, then the craving fades away.

Final Thoughts

Beating procrastination is all about experimenting with different methods to find one that suits you best. It's a complicated problem and different solutions work for different people. My aim in writing this book was to offer you an array of tools to first recognize, and then beat the enemy. To help you finish what you started. Regardless of the issue, I've always felt dissatisfied only reading a list of solutions without the explanation of the problem. That's why I thought it was fundamental to explore and understand the roots of procrastination before tackling it. Imagine bringing your bike to a repair shop because of a flat tire. The person attending you could inflate it in two seconds. But if the tire was actually punctured, a pump would only solve the problem for the time being. Similarly, if you don't get to the root of a problem, you will likely be stuck forever with band-aid fixes.

Identifying your specific type and employing the appropriate strategy to fight it, you'll get rid of procrastination. However, unless you make an active effort to maintain your new habits, you will find yourself back to square one after a few weeks. Like any other skill, you need to keep sharpening the sword and practicing the methods you've learned to make sure old habits won't come back to haunt you. But no worries, I've got you covered. Let's move on to the final chapter.

Key Takeaways

1. There is no single solution to procrastination. Different personality types require different solutions.
2. For Type 1, break big tasks into smaller, more manageable ones, learn to prioritize, eliminate bottlenecks and reduce the number of decisions that you have to make.
3. For Type 2, increase self-efficacy, surround yourself with positive people, don't be afraid to ask for help, avoid chasing after perfectionism and know your fears.
4. For Type 3, keep yourself motivated by setting reasonable deadlines, rewarding yourself when you achieve a milestone, visualizing yourself succeeding and staying focused on the end prize.

Finding out your productivity cycle, delaying gratification when you seem to give in to impulses, getting in the flow, organizing yourself and following a fixed work routine are some additional methods that can help you fend off procrastination.

CHAPTER SEVEN: YOU DON'T HIT THE GYM ONCE AND GET A SIX PACK

> *"Motivation is what gets you started. Habit is what keeps you going."*
>
> — Jim Rohn

This may be the most important chapter of the book. Because yes, you can understand why you behave the way you do and find a solution. But if you don't stick to it, you'll be back procrastinating in no time... with the added frustration that you had been free from it for a while.

I have to confess it took me ages to understand this last piece of the puzzle and to implement it. It wasn't until a friend of mine challenged me to write things down for 30 days that I realized it made the difference between staying procrastination-free or getting back to postponing. Yes, you read it well: *write things down.*

I began writing down a to-do list, trying to stick to it daily; then I also added my notes. I kept adjusting my write-ups until, by the end of the month, I had something that not only kept me going, but helped me understand where I was going wrong. In the end, I asked myself how I hadn't thought about it before: a mix of a journal and a to-do list with my own tweaks. Hence, I urge you to read through this small chapter and start using The JournaList (that's how I called it: a mix between a journal and a to-do list). So many times we read actionable sections in books, but don't act, thinking that what we read was already enough to pick up new habits or change our lifestyle for good. But, in reality, this is where all the difference is made. I'm so sure about it, that I'm explaining in details how you can craft your own JournaList, and how to get one for free.

The DIY Option

If you're a pen and paper person or you just enjoy crafting your own things, you can follow these easy steps and create your own JournaList.

Step 1: On the top-left corner of the page, add the **date** and, next to it, your **long-term goal**.

Step 2: Below add your **Priority list** for the day. Whether you are working on a college assignment, a personal project, or a work activity, add the to-do list of items here. How to compile it to achieve the best results? You should order the items following Gary Keller's *ONE thing* concept: *"what's the ONE thing you can do such that by doing it, everything else will be easier or unnecessary?"*

Step 3: As I stated often in the book, procrastination is an emotion-regulation issue. Hence, below the Priority list, you should add a **Where/Why do I Get Stuck?** section. Throughout the day, you should note here where (i.e. Doing precisely what?) you feel the need to stop working and looking for a distraction. That's where you understand exactly what's stopping you. You need to write it down, so you'll know how to deal with it, using the solutions provided in the earlier chapters (e.g. Are you feeling overwhelmed and need to split tasks into smaller ones? Do you need to remind yourself about the goal? Etc.).

Step 4: Next, you need to add a **Distraction** list. Remember when earlier in the book I mentioned my bullet-proof method that was so easy, so laughable, yet so powerful? It's something I recently came up with, which saved me - and still is - hours and hours every single day. And it works like this: let's say you're researching a topic online for your assignment, you'll surely come across an endless list of potential distractions (links to other websites, news, videos, etc.). Or perhaps you suddenly remember you need to pay the electricity bill. Or something less urgent, such as 'What's the name of the blonde actress from Kill Bill?' The fix is to write down every single item your mind comes up with, for you to check later. Doing this, you won't interrupt your flow, but will keep the focus on what you're working on. Once you're finished for the day, you can get back to this list and check/do everything's on it all at once.

Please, don't dismiss it just because it sounds too simple. You'll be surprised to realize most items aren't important at all. (And by the way, the actress is of course Uma Thurman!)

Step 5: Lastly, you add an **End of Day Notes** section, to reflect on your progress or simply to check where you should improve.

Now that you've created your own JournaList, how should you use it? Here are my suggestions: you can add the date at any time, this is just to track your progress; you should fill the Priority List in the evening after dinner, so, when you get up the following day, you don't have to worry about what needs to be done.

The Long-term goal should be written down every morning as you're starting your work-day. Remember when I mentioned the episodic future thinking? When you write your long-term goal, spend a few moments imagining the future. You need to take full responsibility for your goal and your future, knowing it's going to be You that will enjoy the achievement. And it's still you that will stress over what hasn't been achieved. Have a quick conversation with your future self and listen to what that person has to say: let her or him convince you to achieve your goal.

The Stuck and Distraction sections should be filled as you go throughout the day. And the End of Day Notes... well, at the end of the day.

The FREE Option

You can get a FREE JournaList by posting a pic of your copy of Finish What You Started and your favorite quote from the book with the hashtags #TheJournaList and #FinishWhatYouStarted on Instagram, Twitter or Facebook. Then send me a screenshot/link with your name and address (at freejournalistcopy@gmail.com) and wait for your JournaList to arrive!

The Ready-Made Option

The JournaList is also on sale on Amazon, just search for "The JournaList Matt Rosen" or simply scan this QR code:

The layout of the JournaList may seem simple, but filling it every day isn't. That's the hard part. Remember that **consistency** is what ultimately makes all the difference.

Trust me, this is life changing.

CONCLUSION

"Procrastination has been called a thief—the thief of time. I wish it were no worse than a thief. It is a murderer; and that which it kills is not time merely, but the immortal soul."

— William Nevins

1934, Pennsylvania. Businessman and philanthropist Edgar Kauffman commissioned the renowned American architect, Frank Lloyd Wright, to design a house. Wright delayed working on the design and jumped out of his seat when he learned of Kauffman's surprise visit to his house in September 1935. As his nervous servants looked on, Wright grabbed a pen and paper and managed to draw the design in the time that it took Kauffman to arrive. The house he designed was named Fallingwater and was a huge success.

It didn't take long for it to achieve the prestigious status of a National Historic Landmark.

The acclaimed English writer Samuel Johnson set off to write a new edition of Shakespeare's plays and took almost ten years to complete it. Another famous writer, Samuel Taylor Coleridge, left his widely known poem, Kubla Khan, incomplete due to "the arrival on his door of a person of business from Porlock." An excuse that many believe was intended to cover up his opium addiction.

Procrastination, however, is not a vice limited to individuals with loose morals. The 14th Dalai Lama, Tenzin Gyatso, who lives a life of simplicity and travels the world teaching people to be compassionate and kind, struggled with procrastination as a student. "Only in the face of a difficult challenge or an urgent deadline would I study and work without laziness," he remembers.

Delaying important tasks to indulge in things you love may seem harmless. Yet, this seemingly innocent habit can spiral out of control and cripple life for many adults. It can lead to higher levels of stress, weight gain, decreased performance at work, and a host of medical problems. Chronic procrastination should not be taken lightly, as it can cost you a lot in terms of your mental, emotional, and physical health.

The first step for getting rid of procrastination involves self-reflection; I can't stress this enough. Once you identify the unique triggers and distractions you engage in, you can work out an effective strategy to change your unproductive habits. However, you must remember that change doesn't happen overnight. As you embark on your journey to get rid of procrastination, arm yourself with a lot of patience and perseverance. It is a slow journey, but it might change your life forever. Just imagine how much you would accomplish if you could finish what you started. Launch your own business, lose weight, get a degree... the list is endless.

As we learned in this book, one major reason for procrastination is a lack of self-confidence and self-esteem that disrupts our emotion regulation process. That's why we need to heal our distorted self-image, gain confidence, conquer our fears, and realistically evaluate our abilities. Getting over this harmful habit means repairing your relationship with your Self. It is a personal journey of rediscovering who you are.

Learning about famous procrastinators and their remarkable achievements is a double-edged sword. Leonardo da Vinci may have left behind an unparalleled legacy while doodling in his notebooks, and Frank Lloyd Wright could draw the design of a building that would go on to become a historical landmark within a few hours. But is it wise for you to try your luck and leave things for the last minute, hoping to discover your latent genius?

Let's look at one final story of another famous procrastinator: Colonel Johann Rall, the German commander of the Hessians, at the Battle of Trenton. During the American War of Independence, George Washington and his troops crossed the Delaware River and planned to ambush the Hessians. Some people believe that Rall was given a note, telling him about George Washington's plans, while he was engrossed in a game of cards. Favoring short-term pleasures amid a time where concentration was highly required. Washington's forces launched a surprise attack the next morning, defeating the Hessians. Rall was found lying dead on the battlefield after a musket ball struck him in the head. The note was found in his pocket, still unopened.

So, while there is a slight chance you might end up achieving eternal glory while procrastinating, it's a risk that's frankly not worth taking. Imagine if Elon Musk, J.K. Rowling, Albert Einstein or Oprah Winfrey were all dysfunctional procrastinators. How many things would have we missed? Sadly, we don't know how much great work was left unfinished because of procrastinators. Please, don't be one of them. Don't be forgotten. Finish what you started.

MY LITTLE ASK

If you enjoyed the book, it would mean the world to me if you could leave a review on Amazon!

Reviews help other readers find books, and help (first-time) authors spreading their work.

If you didn't like the book, please let me know your thoughts and comments at hello@self-improvement.me

Either way, thank you for reading Finish What You Started!

ACKNOWLEDGMENTS

I wish to thank my dear friend Jared for inspiring me to write this book and suggesting I *wrote things down*. Also, a special thank you to Karima, Jordan and Mike for being amazing beta readers and, in a way, *bullet*-proof-readers.

Thanks to my editor Jean for her patience and her brilliant work. Kudos to all the academic researchers who have dedicated their lives to study procrastination, offering us explanations and practical solutions. If there are errors with the research/theories I quoted in this book, it's obviously my fault for not reporting them correctly, not theirs.

Lastly, a huge thanks to my family for their support and encouragement, and to Stella, for having let me disappear while I was writing (and re-writing), without ever making me feel like a bad person. Without you all, I would have never finished what I started: this book.

IF YOU HAVEN'T ALREADY...
WANT THESE 2 EBOOKS FOR FREE?

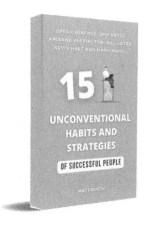

15 Unconventional Habits and Strategies of Successful people
(Oprah Winfrey, Jeff Bezos, Arianna Huffington, Bill Gates...)

No More Distractions: The Easy Trick That Will Stop You From Getting Distracted

To Download the FREE ebooks just scan the QR code:

if the code doesn't work, please email hello@self-improvement.me

BIBLIOGRAPHY

Alexander, E. S., & Onwuegbuzie, A. J. (2007, May). Academic procrastination and the role of hope as a coping strategy. *Personality and Individual Differences, 42*(7), 1301 - 1310. https://doi.org/10.1016/j.paid.2006.10.008

Archontaki, D., Lewis, G. J., & Bates, T. C. (2013, April). Genetic influences on psychological well-being: A nationally representative twin study. *Research output: Contribution to journal, 81*(3), 221-230. https://doi.org/10.1111/j.1467-6494.2012.00787.x

Ariely, D., & Heyman, J. (2004, December https://www.researchgate.net/publication/8234759_Effort_for_Payment_A_Tale_of_Two_Markets). Effort for Payment A Tale of Two Markets. *Journal of Psychological Science, 15*(11), 787 - 793. 10.1111/j.0956-7976.2004.00757.x

Bregman, P. (2010, February 3). *A Story About Motivation*. Harvard Business Review. Retrieved October 1, 2021, from https://hbr.org/2010/02/a-story-about-motivation.html

Brewer, J. (2020, May 19). *Are You Stuck in the Anxiety-Distraction Feedback Loop?* Harvard Business Review. Retrieved October 2, 2021, from https://hbr.org/2020/05/are-you-stuck-in-the-anxiety-distraction-feedback-loop

Bui, N. H. (2007). Effect of Evaluation Threat on Procrastination Behavior. *The Journal of Social Psychology, 147*(3), 197 - 209. https://doi.org/10.3200/SOCP.147.3.197-209

Cherry, K. (2021, July 28). *The 6 Stages of Behavior Change.* Very Well Mind. Retrieved October 15, 2021. https://www.verywellmind.com/the-stages-of-change-2794868

Clear, J. (2020). *Procrastination: A Scientific Guide on How to Stop Procrastinating.* James Clear. Retrieved September 29, 2021, from https://jamesclear.com/procrastination

Currey, M. (2018). Daily rituals. Macmillan.

Currey, M. (2020, March 30). *Was Leonardo da Vinci a Procrastinator?* Subtle Maneuvers. Retrieved September 1, 2021. https://masoncurrey.substack.com/p/was-leonardo-da-vinci-a-procrastinator

Cutuli, D. (2014, September 19). Cognitive reappraisal and expressive suppression strategies role in the emotion regulation: an overview on their modulatory effects and neural correlates. *Frontiers in Systems Neuroscience.* https://doi.org/10.3389/fnsys.2014.00175

Domaradzka, E., & Fajkowska, M. (2018, June 12). Cognitive Emotion Regulation Strategies in Anxiety and Depression Understood as Types of Personality. *Frontiers in Psychology.* https://doi.org/10.3389/fpsyg.2018.00856

Du Plessis, D. (n.d.). *Procrastination And Fatigue? A Deadly Combination*. Online Resources. Retrieved October 3, 2021. https://www.streetdirectory.com/etoday/-wpuewo.html

Duru, E., & Balkis, M. (2019, February 23). Procrastination and Rational/Irrational Beliefs: A Moderated Mediation Model. *Journal of Rational-Emotive & Cognitive-Behavior Therapy, 37*, 299-315. https://doi.org/10.1007/s10942-019-00314-6

Eckert, M., Ebert, D. D., Lehr, D., Sieland, B., & Berking, M. (2016, December). Overcome procrastination: Enhancing emotion regulation skills reduce procrastination. *Learning and Individual Differences, 52*(December), 10 - 18. https://doi.org/10.1016/j.lindif.2016.10.001

Famous Procrastinators. (n.d.). Procrastination and Science. Retrieved September 5, 2021, from https://procrastinus.com/procrastination/famous-procrastinators/

Ferrari, J. R. (2001, September 1). Procrastination as self-regulation failure of performance: effects of cognitive load, self-awareness, and time limits on 'working best under pressure'. *European Journal of Personality, 15*(5), 391-406. https://doi.org/10.1002/per.413

Foroux, D. (2019, June 17). *Procrastination Study: 88% Of The Workforce Procrastinates*. Darius Foroux. Retrieved September 7, 2021, from https://dariusforoux.com/procrastination-study/

Gimming, D., Huguet, P., Caverni, J.-P., & Cury, F. (2006, December). Choking under pressure and working memory capacity: When performance pressure reduces fluid intelligence. *Psychonomic Bulletin and Review, 13*, 1005-1010. https://doi.org/10.3758/BF03213916

Griffey, H. (2018, October 14). *The lost art of concentration: being distracted in a digital world*. The Guardian. Retrieved October 3, 2021, from https://www.theguardian.com/lifeandstyle/2018/oct/14/the-lost-art-of-concentration-being-distracted-in-a-digital-world

Hagen, E. (1990). Advanced techniques for film scoring. Alfred Music.

Hargreaves, S. (2013, July 29). *Why we're working less than our parents did.* CNN Business. Retrieved September 10, 2020, from https://money.cnn.com/2013/07/29/news/economy/working-fewer-hours/index.html

Harvard Health Publishing. (2021, February 12). *4 ways to boost your self-compassion.* Harvard Health Publishing. Retrieved October 20, 2021, from https://www.health.harvard.edu/mental-health/4-ways-to-boost-your-self-compassion

Here's What Happens When You Don't Get Enough Sleep (And How Much You Really Need a Night) Sleep needs by age group. (2020, July 16). Cleveland Clinic: Health Essentials. Retrieved September 7, 2021, from https://health.clevelandclinic.org/happens-body-dont-get-enough-sleep/

Jaffe, E. (2013, March 29). *Why Wait? The Science Behind Procrastination.* Association for Psychological Science. Retrieved September 4, 2021, from https://www.psychologicalscience.org/observer/why-wait-the-science-behind-procrastination

Klassen, R. M., Krawchuk, L. L., & Rajani, S. (2008, October). Academic procrastination of undergraduates: Low self-efficacy to self-regulate predicts higher levels of procrastination. *Contemporary Educational Psychology, 33*(4), 915 - 931. https://doi.org/10.1016/j.cedpsych.2007.07.001

Lally, P., Van Jaarsveld, C. H. M., Potts, H. W. W., & Wardle, J. (2010, October). How are habits formed: Modelling habit formation in the real world. *European Journal of Social Psychology, 40*(6), 998-1009. https://doi.org/10.1002/ejsp.674

Lavoie, J. A., & Pychyl, T. A. (2001, November 1). Cyberslacking and the Procrastination Superhighway: A Web-Based Survey of Online Procrastination, Attitudes, and Emotion. *Social Science Computer Review, 19*(4), 431-444. https://doi.org/10.1177/089443930101900403

Lay, C. H., Edwards, J. M., & Parker, J. D. A. (1989, September 1). An assessment of appraisal, anxiety, coping, and procrastination during an examination period. *The European Journal of Personality, 3*(3), 195 - 208. https://doi.org/10.1002/per.2410030305

Leiberman, C. (2019, March 25). *Why You Procrastinate (It Has Nothing to Do With Self-Control)*. The New York Times. Retrieved September 10, 2021, from https://www.nytimes.com/2019/03/25/smarter-living/why-you-procrastinate-it-has-nothing-to-do-with-self-control.html

Liberman, N., & Trope, Y. (2010). Construal-level theory of psychological distance. *Psychological Review, 117*(2), 440 - 463. https://doi.org/10.1037/a0018963

Metin, U. B., Peters, M. C.W., & Taris, T. W. (2018, July 19). Correlates of procrastination and performance at work: The role of having "good fit". *Journal of Intervention and Prevention in the Community, 46*(3), 228-244. https://doi.org/10.1080/10852352.2018.1470187

Milgram, N., Marshevsky, S., & Sadeh, C. (1994, May 4). Correlates of Academic Procrastination: Discomfort, Task Aversiveness, and Task Capability. *The Journal of Psychology, 129*(2), 145 - 155. https://doi.org/10.1080/00223980.1995.9914954

Neff, K. (2015). Self-Compassion. William Morrow.

Nguyen, B., Steel, P., & Ferrari, J. R. (2013, December). Procrastination's Impact on the Workplace and the Workplace's Impact on Procrastination. *International Journal of Selection and Assessment, 21*(4), 388 - 399. 10.1111/ijsa.12048

Onwuegbuzie, A. J., & Daley, C. E. (1999, June 1). Perfectionism and statistics anxiety. *Perfectionism and Statistics Anxiety*, *26*(6), 1089 - 1102. https://doi.org/10.1016/S0191-8869(98)00214-1

Perry, J. (2012). The Art of Procrastination. Workman Publishing Company.

Psychological distance. (2021, June 21). Wikipedia. Retrieved September 29, 2021, from https://en.wikipedia.org/wiki/Psychological_distance

Pychyl, T., & Sirois, F. (2013). Procrastination and the Priority of Short-Term Mood Regulation: Consequences for Future Self. *Social and Personality Psychology Compass*, *7*(2), 115-127. 10.1111/spc3.12011

Pychyl, T., & Sirois, F. (2013, February 7). Procrastination and the Priority of Short-Term Mood Regulation: Consequences for Future Self. *Social and Personality Psychology Compass*, *7*(2), 115 - 127. https://doi.org/10.1111/spc3.12011

Pychyl, T. A., & Ferrari, J. R. (2007, March). Regulating speed, accuracy and judgments by indecisives: Effects of frequent choices on self-regulation depletion. *Personality and Individual Differences*, *42*(4), 777 - 787. https://doi.org/10.1016/j.paid.2006.09.001

Rabin, M., & O'Donoghue, T. (2000, March 29). The economics of immediate gratification. *Journal of Behavioral Decision Making*, *13*(2), 233 - 250. https://doi.org/10.1002/(SICI)1099-0771(200004/06)13:2<233::AID-BDM325>3.0.CO;2-U

Rana, B. (2020, December 29). *What Are The Ways To Overcome The Lack of Perseverance?* Rana Heals. Retrieved October 3, 2021, from https://ranaheals.com/what-are-the-ways-to-overcome-the-lack-of-perseverance/

Seneca (2005). On the Shortness of Life. Penguin Books.

Sirios, F. M., Melia-Gordon, M. L., & Pychyl, T. A. (2003, October). "I'll look after my health, later": an investigation of procrastination and health. *Personality and Individual Differences*, *35*(5), 1167-1184. https://doi.org/10.1016/S0191-8869(02)00326-4

Sirois, F. M. (2019, March 15). Self-Compassion and Bedtime Procrastination: an Emotion Regulation Perspective. *Mindfulness*, *10*, 434-445. https://doi.org/10.1007/s12671-018-0983-3

Steel, P. (2007). The nature of procrastination: A meta-analytic and theoretical review of quintessential self-regulatory failure. *Psychological Bulletin*, *133*(1), 65-94. https://doi.org/10.1037/0033-2909.133.1.65

Stillman, J. (2020, March 24). *'Handmaid's Tale' Author and Self-Described Lazy Person Margaret Atwood Explains How She Beats Procrastination*. Inc. Retrieved October 2, 2021, from https://www.inc.com/jessica-stillman/handmaids-tale-author-self-described-lazy-person-margaret-atwood-explains-how-she-beats-procrastination.html

Sun-tzu (2009). The Art of War. Penguin Classics.

Tice, D. M., & Bratslavsky, E. (2000). Giving in to Feel Good: The Place of Emotion Regulation in the Context of General Self-Control. *Journal of Psychological Inquiry*, *11*(3), 149 - 159. https://doi.org/10.1207/S15327965PLI1103_03

Vozza, S. (2015, August 7). *8 Myths You Probably Believe About Procrastination*. Fast Company. Retrieved September 10, 2021, from https://www.fastcompany.com/3048087/8-myths-you-probably-believe-about-procrastination

Wainwright, M. (2005, April 22). *Emails 'pose threat to IQ'*. The Guardian. Retrieved October 2, 2021, from https://www.theguardian.com/technology/2005/apr/22/money.workandcareers

Weller, C. (2014, June 5). *Is Procrastination Causing Your Sleep Deprivation? The Dangers Of Pushing Back Your Bedtime.* Medical Daily. Retrieved September 7, 2021, from https://www.medicaldaily.com/procrastination-causing-your-sleep-deprivation-dangers-pushing-back-your-bedtime-286568

Weller, C. (2017, November 18). *Americans work less than ever before but still feel like there's no free time — and there's a simple explanation.* Insider. Retrieved September 9, 2021, from https://www.businessinsider.com/why-it-feels-like-you-have-no-free-time-anymore-2017-11

Wohl, M. J.A., Pychyl, T. A., & Bennett, S. H. (2010, May). I forgive myself, now I can study: How self-forgiveness for procrastinating can reduce future procrastination. *Personality and Individual Differences, 48*(7), 803 - 808. https://doi.org/10.1016/j.paid.2010.01.029

Yan, W.-S., Zhang, R.-R., Lan, Y., Li, Z.-M., & Li, Y.-H. (2018, April 26). Questionnaire-Based Maladaptive Decision-Coping Patterns Involved in Binge Eating Among 1013 College Students. *Frontiers in Psychology.* https://doi.org/10.3389/fpsyg.2018.00609

Made in the USA
Coppell, TX
19 May 2022